Unbreakable
THREADS

Unbreakable
THREADS

THE TRUE STORY OF AN AUSTRALIAN MOTHER, A REFUGEE BOY AND WHAT IT REALLY MEANS TO BE A FAMILY

EMMA ADAMS

ALLEN&UNWIN
SYDNEY·MELBOURNE·AUCKLAND·LONDON

To our parents

First published in 2018

Copyright © Emma Adams 2018

The author acknowledges Denise Leith, for her editorial coaching and mentorship

Allen & Unwin
83 Alexander Street
Crows Nest NSW 2065
Australia
Phone: (61 2) 8425 0100
Email: info@allenandunwin.com
Web: www.allenandunwin.com

 A catalogue record for this book is available from the National Library of Australia

ISBN 978 1 76063 310 3

Set in 12.5/18 pt Fairfield by Midland Typesetters, Australia
Printed and bound in Australia by Griffin Press

10 9 8 7 6 5 4 3 2

 The paper in this book is FSC® certified. FSC® promotes environmentally responsible, socially beneficial and economically viable management of the world's forests.

CONTENTS

Preface   xi

  1 Wickham Point   1
  2 Witnessing   7
  3 Not turning away   16
  4 A mother's dilemma   20
  5 Grasping the thread   26
  6 Rob's family   31
  7 A letter to Abdul   37
  8 How indefinite feels   40
  9 A letter to Scott Morrison   46
 10 The invisible threat   52
 11 Letters from my sons   56
 12 The back-up plan   60

13	The second visit	64
14	Despair	69
15	Birds	73
16	The happiest kid in detention	78
17	The third visit	88
18	A special visitor	93
19	Data breach	99
20	Wings	104
21	A letter to Zaynab	107
22	Waiting at the airport	112
23	Freedom isn't just walking out the door	116
24	Our ancestors' wounds	121
25	The Corn Trail	128
26	The face of the immigration department	134
27	Boys reunited	138
28	Connecting	141
29	Watching television	148
30	Food	151
31	Faith	158
32	Magic carpets	162
33	Family pride	165
34	Growing pains	170
35	Ahad the stout-hearted	177
36	A moment of delight	184
37	Running	189
38	ID tags	193
39	Parenting against the odds	197

Contents

40 Remembering   206

41 Visas   213

42 The 'Fast-Track' interview   217

43 Shoulder surgery   226

44 He's getting younger   230

45 The assault   233

46 Language   242

47 The Emma and Abdul show   247

48 One of us   264

49 A horrible realisation   268

50 Kindness   272

51 The worst just keeps happening   278

52 Seeing refugees on boats   281

53 Leila and Ali   287

54 Loving and letting go   293

55 Wadbilliga   298

56 Hope   303

57 The mountain—an allegory   310

58 Happiness   317

Afterword   321

Acknowledgements   323

PREFACE

Throughout our lives, the many threads of a story are woven simultaneously. No one's sense of self is constant; instead it is held together within a web of memories and feelings. When two or more people are involved in our story, what happens in the 'in-between' becomes more complex. Who we love and live with changes us. Who we meet and how we interact with them changes us. Love and joy and hurt and loss *all* change us. Every day, different truths of our selves are revealed. It is only in retrospect that a story can truly be seen. What I knew then and what I know now are worlds apart.

This is the story of how two Hazara brothers, Abdul and Ahad, who fled horrors in Afghanistan in the hope of safety in Australia, came to join our family and how this changed all of us.

I can't presume to tell their story in full as it is not mine to tell, but you will learn something of why they are here in Australia and what happened to them along the way. You will also learn how they came to be part of our family, and how Australia's immigration policies affect the lives of not only people seeking peace and safety here—people like Abdul and Ahad—but of ordinary Australians like my family. For these beautiful Afghan boys could be any of our children.

Our story is told through a patchwork of observations, pictures of our day-to-day life at home, letters, diary entries and Facebook messages, and in this telling I will share with you what I have learned about love, acceptance and the inter-action of cultures.

Love—this most complex of all emotions—can give us more strength and tenacity than we could ever have thought possible.

IMPORTANT NOTE

This book concerns people who are in uncertain situations, who may remain at risk, or whose families are at risk. Although identifying data in many cases has been removed or changed for safety and privacy, the truth of their stories remains unchanged.

Chapter 1

WICKHAM POINT

We drive 40 kilometres south from Darwin along a flat, scrubby road to reach an isolated peninsula. It is surrounded by swamp and a cluster of buildings sits on a red gash of newly cleared ground. Before we are allowed through the security gates, a guard checks our names, IDs and the purpose of our visit. In the car park, we walk past teetering pallets stacked high with baby baths in mouldering cardboard boxes, while high in the harsh blue sky eagles wheel in the tropical thermals. This is the Wickham Point detention centre complex.

Originally earmarked for mining company accommodation, the place was eventually abandoned because of health risks related to the dangerous number of sandflies and mosquitos. Despite these concerns, the Department of

Immigration had recently taken up the lease to accommodate asylum-seeking families.

As we walk across the hot bitumen to the entry point that December of 2013, I try to comprehend what I have been told. Families and over 300 children, including newborn babies, are being held behind that barbed wire. Some children have crossed the sea alone. These are the people I have come to see.

As a psychiatrist specialising in the mental health of mothers and babies, I am here to visit over three days at the request of ChilOut (Children Out of Immigration Detention), a group opposed to the Australian government's practice of mandatory detention of children. I was a last-minute replacement, as the original paediatrician could not make it. My fellow medical traveller is a professor of obstetrics. We have been asked to observe the care and wellbeing of mothers and babies, and the facilities available to them, in immigration detention in and around Darwin.

It is Friday. We are to be given an official tour of Wickham and Blaydin* detention centres, both of which are out of town at a place called Wickham Point along Channel Island Road, and then we are to inspect Darwin Airport Lodge, a detention centre adjacent to the airport. At all times today, we are to be escorted by Department of Immigration public servants and staff from Serco, the British multinational company contracted to run the centres. Over the weekend, we will sit down and talk with some of the families that have sought asylum and are now indefinitely detained in this place.

---

* In 2014 the spelling was changed to Bladin.

The Serco employees take us to a tea room and give us a security talk. We are told we should use insect repellent and wear solid, covered shoes because of insects and snakes. The same matter of fact tone is used when they talk about the people we are about to encounter inside. When the perfunctory talk is finished, we have our ID checked again, our bags are X-rayed, and after depositing our phones and electronic devices with security we're swept by metal detectors. We then pass through several sets of locked gates and are escorted along a grim, narrow corridor of welded grilles and through a double layer of electrified wire perimeter fencing until we are finally inside. I can see shipping containers stacked two high; these are the living quarters of Wickham Point. It is what the government calls an 'alternative place of detention', or APOD for short. This is supposed to be the family-friendly version. With electric fences, guards and no freedom to come and go, in reality it is a prison.

In the dining room, I notice a male guard because of his body odour. He has his arms outstretched and is blocking the entrance of two young women in modest Muslim dress. Perhaps he thinks he is playing a game, or they find him attractive, because he appears to be enjoying himself, but I can see that these women are uncomfortable. They can't push past him and they can't tell him off. It's clear that this man has all the power. Eventually the young women give him the smile he is looking for and he lets them through.

That this bullying and sexual intimidation is happening so casually and unremarked upon in front of our official group makes me feel uneasy. I can't help wondering what other boundary violations might be happening when no one is looking.

We walk past an isolated courtyard into an accommodation area and I see a small toddler sitting alone in a sandpit. Things are not right here. It is not normal in any culture for babies this age to be just left alone. Where are his parents and why on earth are the people responsible for the care of these children not doing something about his situation? The child's face is blank and his dark eyes stare into space as he repeatedly flicks the handle of a brightly coloured plastic bucket. I can't help but compare this scene with a photograph I have of my eldest son when he was the same age: Jasper is at the beach, his blue eyes alive and smiling back at us as he pauses in his busy digging with a bucket and spade. The child in front of me is not playing. He is helpless; he can't run away or fight this isolation, and since there is no one around to help soothe his distress he has become frozen and dissociated. As we pass by, one of the immigration officials escorting us laughs, commenting how 'cute' this child is. I am appalled that the custodians don't see this gross abnormality.

Further along, I am told off when I refer to a uniformed Serco employee as a 'guard'. Their official title is 'officer', they insist. The people seeking asylum are referred to as 'clients' (as if they have a choice), 'detainees', or, as I heard during my visit, by their boat numbers. Troublingly, artwork decorating the main office and official hallways is signed with boat numbers, the day's list for medical check-ups has a list of boat numbers instead of names, and the following day, when we request a visit to some families, the Serco officer also refers to these people by their boat numbers. When we ask why they use these inhuman monikers, their breezy excuse is that there are 'too many Hosseins'. Language manipulates meaning and I am beginning to see that the language of the detention centre perpetuates the dehumanisation process. Is this deliberate or merely a reflection of their indifference?

Each detention centre has several laminated signs indicating yoga, playgroups and social groups, but they all look as though they have been put up recently. An immigration officer tells us about the early childhood development program, but a few directed questions lead me to believe that the program is no more than a person with a basic TAFE certificate unlocking a room containing toys once or maybe twice a week. In Blaydin APOD, the toy room appears unused, with most of the toys still in their packaging, while in Wickham APOD, the children's bikes strewn around the cement courtyard still have price tags attached. By the end of the first day, the centres' slick veneers of care and responsibility have already vanished. What we saw was an inflexible and harsh institutional culture.

Our dinner back in Darwin that first night is subdued and we go to bed early. I call my husband, Rob, but I can't tell him anything much because I just don't know what to say. All I want is to hear his voice and to say goodnight to my three boys, aged fourteen, eleven and ten, who have been in my mind all day. They would have been terrified in this place. So would I. Despite the comfortable air conditioning I can't sleep, and spend hours lying in bed staring at the ceiling. Prior to this visit, I hadn't given much thought to immigration detention or the lives of people inside these places. In fact, it had mostly been out of a sense of curiosity that I agreed to come. But at the end of this first day, I am appalled and saddened by the inhumanity of this place, and I haven't yet met the inmates.

The next morning, I go for a run along the waterfront to prepare myself: we are about to return to the compounds to visit the asylum seekers who have chosen to speak with us. I feel a weight of responsibility at the prospect of hearing these stories. What a terrible thing it is for people who have bravely fled persecution, fear and mistrust only to arrive in Australia and be held captive without charge or trial.

Chapter 2

WITNESSING

Not one mother we speak with in Blaydin or Wickham knows about the playgroup or the early childhood development program. They smile when we ask about it, and indicate that this is the usual pattern when visitors, such as ourselves or the Red Cross, arrive. The food apparently also improves during these visits.

I speak with a grieving mother whose three-month-old daughter died at the Royal Darwin Hospital. When she runs back to her room to gather something to show me, her despairing husband tells me how terribly worried he is about her mental health. She returns with her shoebox and shows me the precious contents: photos, baby clothes and a treasured letter of condolence and kindness from an Australian mum who was on the same paediatric ward with her and her baby. I learn this distressed couple are only allowed to visit their daughter's grave once a fortnight, and each time the two guards who accompany them never let them linger for long.

As I listen to this slightly built woman's story, I know her husband's fears are well grounded. She appears physically crushed by her dark torment and speaks as if she lost her child only today. It seems cruel to move on, but we need to give time to everybody. I give her my card—an inadequate gesture, I know—which she places gently into her shoebox.

We meet a mother struggling to feed her twelve-day-old baby girl who has been expressing milk by hand around the clock. My experience of helping new mothers tells me that without help there can be difficulties not just with nutrition but in her developing confidence as a new parent. Despite multiple requests, this woman has still not been given access to a breast pump, which costs almost nothing and can make the difference between successful breastfeeding and a mother being forced to wean her newborn baby. I can't understand this penny-pinching meanness, but soon discover this is not these parents' only concern.

The baby's father tells me that in this mosquito-infested swamp baby clothes are a necessity, but Serco only provided them the day before our visit. The parents show us their baby's skin, which is covered with weeping and infected pustules. They tell us that they have tried to show the lesions to immigration's medical service, International Health and Medical Services (IHMS), a private company that has been contracted to supply health care to the detention centres, but the clinicians have refused to see them.

It is standard medical practice in any Australian hospital for a newborn with such potentially serious medical concerns to be examined by a senior doctor. These parents are distressed: not only does their newborn have feeding problems, she is also at risk of serious infection. And yet there is no alternative medical help and they have no right to a second opinion—or, at this stage, even a *first* opinion. They can't jump the electrified fence to get their baby to a doctor. That these parents are unable to access the basics for their child in medical danger is an additional humiliation and stress during their captivity.

Meeting this family, I feel angry, impotent and scared, but I also feel an obligation to do something. My obstetrician colleague looks aghast, and I am guessing that inside she feels the same way as me. She tells the guards, 'This baby is sick and needs to be seen by a doctor now,' and offers to accompany the family to the onsite medical clinic. But the guards won't allow it.

'How about we write an urgent referral letter,' I suggest. 'We'll put our names and the full alphabet of our qualifications on it, and say a doctor needs to see this baby right now and why. They couldn't possibly refuse that.'

Shortly afterwards the parents return. Through the interpreters they tell us that the nurse read our letter but then, without even removing the baby's clothes to look at the lesions, advised them that she was 'fine' and could see a doctor in two days. By any professional standard, this was an appalling decision.

Typical of the children I meet that day is a teenage boy, Mohammad, who arrived in Australia with his family twelve months ago. I'm impressed by his respectful and thought-ful manner and soon discover he is also proficient in many languages—all learned during his time in detention. I also discover that the guards use him as an unofficial interpreter, and he is often pulled out of bed in the early morning to trans-late for other asylum seekers when they have health issues.

As we sit talking, I notice Mohammad is wearing a red wristband, which he tells me was given to him at school in Darwin. Asylum kids are taken to a school in town, but secondary-school age children are not allowed to attend classes with the Australian children. The wristband has the word 'resilience' etched into it, but I can see that this child is at the end of his: he's burned out, depressed and tells me he has run out of hope for any sort of future.

We meet a family whose father pleads for help for his young toddler who is not eating or sleeping, and who he thinks is depressed. They had taken him to IHMS doctors and mental health only to be told there was nothing wrong with him. But clearly something *is* wrong, and not just with this little boy. His mum's face is desolate and she has the 'thousand-yard stare' typical of the severely traumatised. She doesn't interact with her young son, or the baby she's holding on the edge of her lap, facing away from her.

In fact, throughout the whole afternoon, there is little interaction between mother and baby, no eye contact and no smiles. The toddler tries hard to engage his mother, first by doing a super-animated silly dance in front of her. She does not react. He then reaches over and sweetly cuddles his sibling in his mother's lap. Still nothing. So this little boy, desperate for attention, tries something else: he gives the baby a little bite. When the baby cries, there is still no reaction from the mother towards either child, so the toddler pats the crying baby himself. He then runs over to the translator accompanying us and sits on his lap. Next he approaches me, another stranger, bidding for physical contact. Later I observe him hit his father, who seems just as despondent as his wife. Then, out of the blue, he slaps one of my group: a kindly, smiling woman who had been playing with him.

The indiscriminately affectionate behaviour of the child and his acting out are warning signs of a child not receiving the positive interactions he or she needs. His behaviour puts him at increased risk of being exploited in this place. In fact, the whole family's behaviour is ringing warning bells. As a psychiatrist, I knew that if this mother was in the community she would have been admitted to a psychiatric mother–baby unit because her depression was so severe and the disconnection from her children so problematic. This family should have been referred for parent–infant therapy to help their children's distress and problematic behaviour as well as promote attachment and optimal child development. This family were not getting adequate mental health care and their prognosis in a detention situation devoid of hope was grim.

All of the mothers I met with that day were clinically depressed—we spoke with another mother who, in front of her two school-aged children, declared her regrets that she and her family did not drown at sea.

'It would have been better if I fell in the ocean and sharks ate my body. That is better than this.'

The words chilled me, and her mental state was distant and cut off from any reassurance. Not that we could offer any to this family, who had already spent over a year in various detention centres with no end in sight. One of her children, an exceptionally polite and docile eleven-year-old girl who had ensured everyone had a cup of tea, started crying. Her mother continued to stare ahead blankly, miles away from her weeping daughter.

The stories were confronting. I couldn't make sense of any of this, and in the heat I felt suffocated. I am a mother myself. I don't know how I would manage in a place such as this. I would be scared of the guards abusing their power, I would be scared no one would come to help my children when they needed it, and I would be scared that the people in control had no regard for my children's wellbeing. How could I give my boys hope in a place such as this?

A pregnant woman, whose growing belly made her trousers tight, told us she had been refused a replacement pair. Her husband explained that any time they go to the hospital for an appointment they are made to wait outside in the hot sun for an hour or more until the guards are ready to take them back to the detention centre. They can't sleep properly because late each night and early every morning the centre is woken for a head count.

'They can call me illegal,' she says. 'But don't call my baby illegal.'

Her outspoken resistance is like a breath of fresh air in that depressing place.

XXXXXXX

There was another person I met that day at the Blaydin detention centre. Sometimes, now, if I gaze at him long enough, I can still see glimpses of the boy he was back then.

He is about fifteen years old, wearing long pants and a white T-shirt, so clean it seems to glow. He stands at the back of a group helping some of the adults with translation. In contrast to nearly everyone else, this boy holds himself tall, with his chest and head held high. I sense pride and defiance behind his polite manner. Later, this boy approaches me and introduces himself as Abdul. I learn he is alone here in the camp—a child who had travelled the seas with no family to accompany him—and that he is from Afghanistan. I also learn he is Hazara, a persecuted minority in his country. He has been in detention for five months and his official label is UAM, or unaccompanied minor. Some way into our conversation, he asks me:

'Will I die soon?'

That a teenage boy needs to ask this question floors me. He tells me that he is worried about his heart, which sometimes races too fast, especially when he remembers being caught in a bomb attack in Kabul. Two days ago, he fainted. He has seen other people collapse and die with heart disease and wonders if he might too.

He is also worrying about the surgery he needs to fix his shoulder, which keeps painfully dislocating; he was hit by a car in Kabul. In Afghanistan, surgery can literally be a matter of life and death, and he is concerned that immigration will tell his mother, who is still over there, and she will worry too much. All his concern is for her welfare. All his worry is about her, and he keeps asking me if they will tell her.

I explain that I just don't know because I don't work here, but I think to myself, *Poor kid, of course they won't, they'll only tell her if something goes wrong because they don't give a stuff about you or your mother.*

Abdul says he wants to become an economist. From my limited knowledge of this field and of Afghanistan, I think this is an unusual choice for a child of his background and I ask him why. Abdul tells me that if he knows how money moves around the world it might provide an answer to how the world works and why wars happen, and if he has those answers then maybe he could stop people from suffering.

xxxxxxx

There is an eeriness in a system where young people, children, babies and families are held in endless captivity without trial or conviction for any crime. The main sense among the asylum seekers we meet is hopelessness and a stultifying sense of nothingness. These people knew they were going to be detained in one of the mainland detention centres, or offshore on Christmas Island or Nauru, for years and possibly forever because they could never return to the places from which they had fled. They had no other options.

I was told the same story by several women that weekend. It was not a dramatic story but it stuck with me because it summed up the dwindling compassion of the place. On the fortnightly excursions outside the detention centres, the guards sometimes ate ice creams in front of the kids, telling them that no money had been provided for the children to have one. I couldn't believe that the guards could have been so indifferent or that the authorities had not seen fit to provide this small treat for children trapped in the tropics.

As we left, the cognitive dissonance of a guard breezily chirping, 'Hope you enjoyed your visit,' made me wonder just how desensitised the employees of this place had become.

The flight back to Canberra was bumpy and my colleague flying back with me put her hand on mine reassuringly.

'It's not just the turbulence.' I blinked through tears. 'It's what we saw.'

When I arrived back in Canberra, I gave each of my three sleeping boys a kiss. I told Rob what I had seen. He asked me to explain the confusing acronyms and jargon and wanted me to clarify what I had told him because he was so shocked at its awfulness. As I went to bed that night, I hoped I would wake up and find that the last three days at Wickham Point had been a dream.

Chapter 3

NOT TURNING AWAY

In all our lives there are turning points. Before the trip to Darwin, I thought that Australia had a reasonable approach to human rights, but what I saw threw all that into question.

I returned from the detention centres feeling sad and angry, and a defiance grew. I could not forget what I had witnessed and turn away. These people, and especially Abdul, would not leave my mind. Their hopeless predicaments haunted my dreams. I needed to understand what was really going on and to do that I needed to educate myself, beginning with understanding the difference between 'refugee' and 'asylum seeker'.

According to the 1951 United Nations Convention Relating to the Status of Refugees, a refugee is a person who 'owing to a well-founded fear of being persecuted for reasons of race, religion, nationality, membership of a particular social group, or political opinion, is outside the country of his nationality, and is unable or, owing to such fear, is unwilling to avail himself of the protection of that country'.

An 'asylum seeker', on the other hand, is a person who has arrived in a country seeking protection as a 'refugee' but whose claim for refugee status has not yet been assessed by the United Nations or by a country such as Australia, which, as a signatory to the Refugee Convention, is obliged to process asylum seekers when they arrive on our shores.

It seemed straightforward enough to me: an asylum seeker arrives in a country seeking protection in the hope that they will be given refugee status. This brought me to the most dishonest and inherently cruel word in the debate about asylum seekers in Australia: 'illegal'. It is not illegal for a person to cross borders without a visa if they are seeking asylum from persecution. Why does our government call these people illegal when, clearly, they are not? Illegal implies that these so-called 'boat people' are guilty of something, always unnamed, thus making them deserving of poor treatment such as incarceration without trial. The government manipulates this word to demonise and dehumanise asylum seekers, to sway public opinion in the government's favour and to excuse the most callous behaviour imaginable. It is not illegal to seek asylum.

The people locked up in detention centres and offshore processing centres have committed no crime by arriving on our shores. In fact, it is our government—through the practice of indefinite incarceration, removing people offshore, sending boats back and locking up children—that has turned its back on the humanitarian conventions it professes to uphold. Australia now has a seat on the United Nations Human Rights Council and sadly is not adhering to either the United Nations Convention on the Rights of the Child or the Convention Against Torture and Other Cruel, Inhuman or Degrading Treatment or Punishment.

In November 2012, the Gillard government reopened the offshore detention centres of John Howard's 'Pacific Solution' on Manus Island in Papua New Guinea and Nauru, both developing countries. On 19 July 2013, the Rudd government announced that all asylum seekers who arrived by boat on our shores would automatically be sent to either Manus Island or Nauru, and those eventually found to be genuine refugees would be settled elsewhere. No boat arrivals, even if found to be refugees, would ever be allowed to settle in Australia.

Some of the families we met in the Darwin detention centres had arrived in Australia prior to this change of policy and were still waiting for their refugee claims to be processed. There were also those who had arrived after the legislation had been passed: pregnant women brought back from Nauru for safer births and those with medical conditions that could only be attended to in Australia. This last group faced removal back to Nauru and Manus Island as soon as they were deemed fit to travel.

The government argues that this policy of offshore detention is to stop the people-smuggling trade and deaths at sea. All this sounds rational and reasonable—until we realise that this means locking up men, women and children in appalling

conditions with no hope of release. Jailed convicted criminals know if and when they will be released, but not asylum
seekers arriving in Australia.

It shocked me to hear our government threatening to jail
doctors, nurses, teachers and social workers if they spoke
out about the conditions in offshore detention centres. As a
doctor working in Australia, I am mandated under the law to
report child abuse if I see it. Until recently in Nauru, I could
have faced a two-year jail sentence for doing so.

Once you have seen the conditions we have subjected
these people to you can never un-see it. If Australia—a
country I once thought of as one of the 'good ones'—treats
vulnerable people in such a fashion, maybe the world truly
is a horrible place and there is no hope. And I began to think
that if Australians could treat other people's children this
way, perhaps sooner or later this heartlessness might extend
to our own.

But something else was disturbing my equilibrium: this
boy, Abdul. I could not let the memory of him go. I wondered
what it must have taken for his mother to put her child on
a boat.

Chapter 4

A MOTHER'S DILEMMA

After the Darwin trip, I wanted my problem—which was the discomfort and inconvenience of having seen people suffer—to go away. But the memory of the young, unaccompanied Abdul stayed with me. There were times in those first months when I directed my anger towards his mother. *What a reckless thing to do to a child*, I thought.

Why would a mother put her child in harm's way like that? It wasn't only the risks involved with the passage in an overcrowded and dilapidated boat run by shonky people-smugglers across the Indian Ocean. Didn't she know, or care, that a teenage boy travelling alone halfway across the world would be vulnerable in so many other ways?

My uncharitable thoughts persisted. Perhaps in Afghanistan, with so much war and violence, life is cheap? Perhaps in

Afghanistan, children were expendable? Maybe their children are not as loved and precious as our children, and maybe because their families are large they have 'spares'? Perhaps Abdul was a 'throwaway' child to be sent out despite the risks of being killed, raped or drowned. Perhaps, if he made it, the rest of his family could get an income from Australia, or even a chance of coming here too . . . by plane?

I believe that is how a lot of Australians still think about asylum seekers, but Abdul's words of concern about his mother showed me the depth of their relationship. What level of desperation would cause a mother to send her beloved son away on such a perilous journey with the understanding that she may never see him again? After educating myself about my country's immigration policies, I needed to educate myself about Afghanistan.

The Hazaras are one of Afghanistan's ethnic minorities and their traditional homelands are in the mountainous central parts of Afghanistan where farming is the main way of life. It is thought that because of their distinctly East Asian appearance, and their separate dialect, they are likely the descendants of Genghis Khan's Mongolian soldiers, who arrived in Afghanistan in the thirteenth century. By the nineteenth century, the Hazaras represented 67 per cent of the Afghan population, but with over a century of racial, religious and politically motivated attacks—including the taking of Hazaras as slaves—they number no more than nine per cent of the population of Afghanistan today.

In the late 1800s, the British-backed Emir of Afghanistan, Abdul Rahman Khan, seeking greater control over the various tribes in order to suppress uprisings, ordered the extermination of all Shia, resulting in the deaths of tens of thousands of Hazaras. The killings and persecution of this group continued throughout the twentieth century, intensifying in the late 1990s with the arrival of the Taliban, who believe the Shia to be infidels.

In September 1998, the Taliban massacred up to 8000 Hazaras and other minorities in the towns of Mazar-i Sharif and Bamiyan, with about 2000 people killed in three days in Mazar-i Sharif alone. The Taliban moved from door to door, searching for Hazaras and shooting, raping and hacking to death men, women and children. The Taliban also herded hundreds of Hazaras into shipping containers and sealed the doors. Nearly all of the prisoners died. In a final mortification, the Taliban would not allow the dead to be buried.

But the Taliban are not the Hazaras' only enemy. Today they are targeted by other fundamentalist terrorist groups, including Al-Qaeda, Lashkar-e-Jhangvi al Alami and, more recently, Daesh (ISIS). In late 2015, Daesh affiliates abducted four men, two women and a nine-year-old girl from Zabul province. After being held captive for almost four weeks, the prisoners were decapitated with razor wire. In June 2016, armed Taliban gunmen took 25 Hazara men and women hostage as they were travelling in the province of Sar-e Pol; to date, only four women and one elderly man have been released. There are also ongoing attacks and disputes over Hazara farming lands by the nomadic and heavily weaponised Kuchi tribes. Despite their appeals to the Afghan government for help, the attacks on Hazara villages continue.

xxxxxxx

A persecuted person usually seeks asylum after they have fled their homeland. Some suggest that refugees who arrive by boat to Australia are 'queue jumpers'. I wanted to know why Abdul arrived by boat and hadn't waited his turn in the queue.

The 'queue' people are referring to is the refugee resettlement program operated through the UNHCR (the United Nations Refugee Agency). Each year, approximately 80,000 places are offered by resettlement countries. Currently, in excess of one million refugees on the UNHCR books are in need of resettlement.

Because the resettlement scheme only covers a tiny portion of refugees worldwide, the UNHCR emphasises that its humanitarian resettlement program should not be the only way a person can seek protection. It expects signatories of the Refugee Convention (Australia included) to give assessment and safe haven to asylum seekers arriving by boat or any other means that are found to be refugees. The convention intends that people should not be penalised because of their manner of entry.

An examination of the Australian Department of Home Affairs website suggests that it is 'unlikely' that a person will be granted a refugee or humanitarian visa if that person is still living in their home country. There may be a chance of resettlement if a person is lucky enough to have a relative in Australia to lodge an application for them here, but in practice success is rare and will take years. What do people do who are in immediate danger? What would you do if the Taliban or Daesh were coming for you and your loved ones?

There are those who complain that people who escape all the way to Australia by boat are 'country shopping' and instead should stop at the first country they come to. For several decades, Hazaras have escaped into neighbouring Pakistan and Iran, but they're still targeted by the same terrorists in Pakistan, while in Iran a deep-seated antipathy to Afghans manifests itself in the poor treatment of refugees. These neighbours of Afghanistan are also not signatories to the United Nations Refugee Convention, so asylum seekers have no pathway to citizenship, nor are they afforded any pro-tections. Malaysia and Indonesia, two of the countries in which asylum seekers often must make stops on their way to Australia, aren't signatories either. As such, there is no ability to start a new life in these countries: refugees are unable to seek official employment, their children are denied education, and the wait for a place in a third country, such as Australia, may be many decades.

If I was fleeing for my life, I know I'd want to keep going until I found somewhere I and my children could finally feel safe and have a future. I also know that I would do anything to save my children. Anything.

When Abdul left Afghanistan, Australia was still fulfilling its international obligations to process asylum seekers who had arrived by boat and settling those with legitimate claims to refugee status. Unfortunately, Abdul arrived on Christmas Island on 8 August 2013, twenty days too late. Now, according to the new rules, he would never be able to settle in Australia. A few weeks later, the government put out an advertisement where an Australian soldier declares, stony-faced: 'No way.

The message is simple: if you come to Australia illegally by boat, there is no way you will *ever* make Australia home.'

xxxxxxx

Abdul's mother must have been beyond desperate to send her sons on such a perilous journey to Australia. *Sons*— because over the next few weeks I learned that Abdul had an older brother who had arrived in Australia by boat some years earlier. I tried to imagine the agonising choice she had to make for her sons: probable death in Afghanistan or a risky journey with people smugglers in a leaky boat. As a mother, I tried to feel the pain and anguish she must have endured in saying goodbye to her boys, probably forever, but it was too painful. I also thought of the remarkable courage of Abdul in taking this journey.

If I was ever in this mother's situation of having to send my children away, I know that I would want someone to look out for them at the other end. And, with that thought, an idea began to grow.

Chapter 5

GRASPING THE THREAD

That our observations (and criticisms) of the Darwin detention centres were to be made public by ChilOut could have been enough. I could have spent my time writing strongly worded letters to the editor, volunteered for refugee groups or raised money by running marathons. But my heart whispered that none of it would do. I had left someone behind when I left that place.

I couldn't let the memory of Abdul go. Was it because of all the people I met he seemed to have kept a spark of defiance despite the odds? Maybe it was the way he cared for his mum that I found so endearing? Or maybe it was simply because he was a boy, just like my sons, and on his own?

Over the following weeks, I became despondent and withdrew into my thoughts. When I saw my boys coming home from school and helping themselves to food out of the fridge, jumping on their bikes for a ride in the bush or calling out to me as they headed off to see their friends down the street, I thought of the wonderful freedom they did not know they had. Each day my thoughts went back to the boy who had none of these freedoms. And unless I did something, Abdul would eventually be sent to Nauru, a secretive place, and from where some horrible stories were beginning to leak out.

One Saturday morning in early 2014, I was sitting at the kitchen table, staring into the garden and nursing a coffee that had gone cold. My husband, Rob, sat down beside me, rubbed my back and asked me what was on my mind. I was nervous about broaching the subject with him because once I asked I knew everything in our lives could change.

'It's about Abdul, isn't it?' he coaxed. In the weeks since I returned he knew all I knew about Abdul. He waited until I replied.

Rob is an easy-going guy. My first impression of him was formed when I overheard a doctor talking to a confused elderly patient. I could hear his polite, patient and caring voice through the curtains of the hospital emergency department. That is how we met over twenty years ago. The second thing that struck me was his tall, lean build. And then his long hair held back in a ponytail, which had curls like a telephone cord that I wanted to thread my little finger through.

And the fourth thing that struck me was the stitches and scabs covering his face. I soon found out they were the result of coming off his bike on a 5 a.m. training ride. Some months before we met, Rob had returned from a bike trip that took him from Alaska down to the Mexican border in a meandering adventure of 8000 kilometres. We discovered that we shared a love of outdoor adventure and Hungarian music. The year before we met I had travelled to Hungary to hear Magyar and gypsy music live.

Rob's unassuming manner belies just how smart he is. He plays it down, explaining his silences as 'I'm not deep, I'm just content.' Rob has been my staunchest ally through three kids, overseas moves and all sorts of challenges in our families. We are a solid couple and he is a gentle, loving and involved father.

That morning, I looked up from my coffee into his eyes.

'I've been thinking that I'd like to try to get Abdul out of detention. He can come and live with us instead.'

There, I thought, *it has been said*. I hurried on, explaining that it would be much healthier for him to be with a family and we had plenty of room to share now that we had moved into a house with a 'spare' bedroom if I cleaned out all of my craft stuff. I also told him my doubts, for there were so many other things to consider. What if I'd made a mistake in assessing his character in the little time I'd spent with him? What about the mix of our cultures and experiences? And what about his mental health? What about his own family? I knew I was trusting my instinct because I didn't have much else to go on. When I stopped talking there was silence.

'Okay,' Rob said at last.

I thought I hadn't heard right and went through the difficulties again.

'Okay,' he repeated. 'We could try.'

'You'll support me in this?'

'I'll support you.'

'What about the boys?'

'It'll be good for them too.'

And that was that. The words were out and I had one part of the answer.

After explaining the situation over dinner, we tentatively asked our three boys what they thought about the idea.

'What did he do?' my youngest, Toby, who was ten, asked when I told them Abdul had been in detention in Darwin for about six months already.

'He hasn't done anything wrong,' Rob explained.

'Why would they do that? Lock him up?' Lucas, the eleven year old, asked.

'The government says it's to stop other people from drowning,' I told them. But they heard the strain in my voice.

Jasper, who was fourteen, declared, 'But that's not fair!'

They all looked at us shocked, mouths not moving. They'd had a protected life and could not imagine any child being treated this way. And so they all said yes. Of course this other boy, this stranger, could live in our house.

xxxxxx

There is an ancient Chinese myth of a magical thread that connects the hearts and spirits of those who share an important story. The thread may stretch or tangle, but regardless of the chaos and complexity of time, place or circumstances, it is unbreakable. I thought of this myth as I went to sleep that night. Maybe this was destiny, maybe it wasn't—either way, I had to grasp this thread. None of us knew what the outcome would be. The chances of getting Abdul out were very small. What we did know was that this was a boy in distress. I thought we could help.

Chapter 6

ROB'S FAMILY

Rob's parents, Sándor and Emma, had escaped into Austria from Hungary in 1966, and after being assessed as refugees by the UNHCR they had a choice of Australia or Canada. Australia's wait was shorter, so Australia it was.

In the 1960s, there weren't the same numbers of refugees coming to Australia as there are today, but the world has changed, and nowadays a person may live their entire life in a refugee camp and never be resettled. When they arrived in 1967, Sándor and Emma were given accommodation at the Matraville Hostel in eastern Sydney, one of the many migrant hostels used to accommodate new Australians from the 1950s until the 1970s. This was the language from that time: 'New Australians'. No doubt there was suspicion and racism, but this label indicated that Australians were prepared to consider these arrivals as their own.

Sándor grew up in Hungary during World War II and he lived in a tiny one-room house with his two brothers and widowed mother who collected mushrooms from the forest to support the family. None of the boys had shoes and their legs were always covered with sores. They never had enough to eat. Sándor's youngest brother lost an eye to the severe cold: he was on the edge of the bed they all shared and closest to the freezing wall. This childhood poverty was not the driver for Sándor and Emma to escape. They escaped for freedom.

I often try to imagine how Sándor and Emma must have felt on reaching Australia, most likely bringing with them the ever-present anxiety of what was happening to the rest of their family back in Hungary. This young couple were in a strange country where they knew no one. They were only just starting to learn English and had almost nothing to their name. When I think of that time, I especially feel for Emma, who was seven months pregnant with Robert. Sándor told us the story of how Emma had labour contractions not long into their flight to Australia and my husband almost arrived mid-air over Afghanistan. Luckily this didn't happen and Rob was born just a few weeks after his parents arrived in Australia.

The migrant hostel was utilitarian and not very pretty, but in this system New Australians were helped to settle into the community. Old photographs of the Matraville Hostel, which was previously a naval storage facility, show a row of tall, pale-coloured weatherboard buildings linked by awnings. The photographs depict families congregated under the awnings and some little children riding tricycles. Along the perimeter of the hostel grounds are half-cylindrical, corrugated-steel Nissen huts.

Rob's christening photos show a scrawny baby lying beside a young woman sitting on a bed. Light streams in through louvred glass windows on to a metal hospital crib. On display is a small photo album in an embroidered Hungarian design, a vase of flowers, a crucifix and a postcard of Heroes' Square in Budapest. It is clear from these photos that Emma has made an effort to decorate this sparse interior with the only possessions they have. Sándor told me when I was looking through the album with him that her dress was bought in Vienna with UN clothing vouchers.

One evening long ago, as Toby slept peacefully in my arms, Sándor told me a story about my husband's earliest days. Robert was an unsettled baby and Emma, who had lost her own mother when she was only a child, was isolated in this new and foreign country. Little was understood about postnatal depression at that time, and with no professional help, or friends or family to offer encouragement and valida- tion, Emma and the baby would often end up crying together.

The partitions between living quarters in the hostel were thin; Sándor was worried that the neighbours would complain. He was also worried about Emma and the baby getting enough sleep. So he decided to put Robert in another room and lock the door, with the wishful thinking that sep- arating a distressed mother and her crying baby would allow each of them to rest. He also told me that baby Robert was fed melted butter when he lost weight. My heart ached for the family. Fortunately, later photographs show a happier, plumper baby giving his smiling mother a sloppy kiss on her cheek. Nevertheless, things must have been grim for this young couple during those early months.

I never met my mother-in-law, but I know it was her love that endowed Rob and his sister, Alice, with such fortitude and kindness. If Emma had not recovered, and had not been able to forge that strong bond with her children, I don't think Rob or Alice would be the people they are today.

Sándor and Emma worked hard to carve out a life in their new land. Although Sándor was an engineer in Hungary, his qualifications were not recognised in Australia, and his first jobs were in factories. Emma, who had an agricultural degree, worked as a house cleaner, with baby Robert sitting quietly near her as she worked. Later, in their own home they nurtured a spectacularly colourful garden from bare earth. Sándor made most of their furniture, while Emma cooked everything from scratch and sewed the family's clothes. On weekends the family would take long excursions around Sydney and into the bush, coining the family phrase 'Another good place!'

Not long after arriving in Australia, Sándor changed his name to Alex, while Bagyinszki, their surname, was also changed to something more Anglo-sounding. Rob and Alice learned English from their parents and from the kids down the street, but their first language was Hungarian. Although the family wanted to assimilate, Emma was keen to ensure that the children retained their culture. They read Hungarian children's stories, ate traditional Hungarian food, learned music the Hungarian way and both children attended traditional Hungarian dance lessons dressed in puffy shirts—much to Rob's discomfit and Alice's delight.

After working so hard for a better life, Sándor did not want to take any more risks. He wanted his family to be safe from poverty, which meant education was paramount. My husband and his sister were pushed to do well at school. Rob wanted to do astrophysics, but this was not considered a 'real' job and so he became a doctor instead.

Rob's family arrived as refugees: as newcomers in a sea of strangers. They were helped and their contributions were valued. This family flourished and have become successful, generous citizens of Australia. And now my husband, the son of refugees, was willing to open our home and family to another refugee who had found his way to our shores.

xxxxxxx

Even if I could not get Abdul out, I believed that the knowledge that I was thinking about him, and that I would try as hard as I could to help, might be the only lifeline he had in that deadening place. The venture would be difficult and I knew all along that if it was going to happen it would be a marathon effort. The only person who was prepared to take this on was me. I knew that I had to push it—and most likely wing it. I hazarded a guess that Abdul would be willing and capable of this venture before I offered it to him. He had already stood out as a risk-taker and a resilient young man.

I also knew Abdul had a brother in Brisbane, but I didn't know if he had any other family here. If he wanted to live

35

with his brother, I hoped he could. But first we had to get him out of detention.

A few weeks after I first met Abdul, I wrote to him. It took some time for the letter to find its way through the network of volunteer visitors I had met when I visited Darwin, but I am so glad it did.

And so it began.

Chapter 7

A LETTER TO ABDUL

Wednesday, 8 January 2014

Dear Abdul

I can't imagine how you must feel stuck where you are. So I apologise if what I offer you in any way makes it more difficult for you.

I am the doctor that came with ChilOut to Darwin in December. You were helping translate for some families, but you also described your situation and concerns about your mother worrying about you and your wish to study economics.

After much reflection and discussion with my family, I felt it would be a no-brainer that you may enjoy staying with our family. I do not know what the chances are, more than if we didn't try at all.

Who are we? You have met me briefly. I know this puts you in a difficult situation as I am a stranger. My husband Rob and I are both doctors. I am a psychiatrist. Rob is an anaesthetist. We have three sons, aged fourteen, eleven and ten. We also have two very friendly dogs.

We live in Canberra, Australia's capital city, but it has only 400,000 people. We have a large house full of books. We are an academic family but also all pretty active. Rob rides a bike. Our sons row, swim and play basketball. I like running through the bush. I run to work past mobs of kangaroos.

Why am I making this offer? It is out of respect to your mother. She has done a lovely job in making such a lovely boy. And as a mother myself, I feel I would like to finish what she has started. You have had way too much worry and stress and responsibility for a sixteen year old. I would like to offer you the chance of a few years of a normal Australian life, the chance to properly go to school, make friends, achieve your academic goals . . . and stay on the mainland! We are a long way from Brisbane, unfortunately, but we will also try to get you seeing your brother. Do you have other family in Australia?

Please take time to think about this. If you agree, I can't guarantee success, but we might have a fighting chance. Please let me know and give me your full name and ID so I can talk with immigration here in Canberra. If you would rather not, that is okay . . . can I help in another way? But please take this as a message of hope and that a lot of us Australians care.

Kind regards,
Emma Adams

A letter to Abdul

PS. Please feel free to ask me any questions, even ones you think might be silly. I have included below how to find me on Facebook because that is what everyone says everyone uses. I understand you get an hour or so in the computer room some days.

Chapter 8

HOW INDEFINITE FEELS

A bdul replied to me via Facebook on 23 January 2014:

> Dear Emma I appreciate and I thought much I got the time
> because I had to thought that the family that I want to join
> what will be my responsibality against them. I decide and
> I am agree if you dont have problem .my full name is and my
> boat ID is (HYN071). Thanks Abdul

With only a few phones in the detention centre for the
hundreds of homesick people, along with the cost of inter-
state phone calls falling to the detainees, the internet seemed
the best option of communication with Abdul. But the kids
were only allowed to access the computer room for a few

hours after 9 p.m., and the time delay between Darwin and Canberra meant that our conversations usually took place around 10.30 p.m. my time. The internet connection from Wickham Point was also sketchy and often dropped out, which made communication slow, a problem exacerbated by Abdul's English and his need to have a dictionary beside him.

Before writing to him, I knew the chances of Abdul being allowed to live with us were low. But what was the alternative? The next destination for this boy was Nauru. After Abdul's Facebook reply, I called the Department of Immigration with my offer to sponsor and billet Abdul. Their response, as expected, was a non-committal and confusing bureaucratic one that offered no hope for any eventual freedom. I could not believe the politics behind the detention of children could be so heartless.

Despite the uncertainty, I messaged Abdul on Facebook each night I could. I wanted this to be a lifeline for him while I worked through the process. Not turning away from this enormous task was mostly all I could do during this long slog as well as occasionally giving healthy life messages to encourage exercise and avoid smoking, alcohol and drugs. Hearing the computer 'ding' announcing Abdul was online and wanted to talk always brightened my evenings. Little by little, we worked out how to communicate and shaped our hopes and dreams of freedom for him and a life in Australia.

Abdul: Hi Emma I can understand you and you have right to worry about your family and I know it s normal but just I want to tell you something that you did your best . . . for me and I never forget this and about the drug and alcohol the last night that I came to here my mom told me that I know your small and this jorney is too hard for you and she told me that never used the alcohol and cegerat and I promise to her and I cant broke my promise.

Emma: Good on you! I agree with your Mum!

Abdul: your right and I know that we dont no each others and know each others just a few months.

Emma: And it is very hard to have the right words and full understanding using Facebook messages. I know you are very strong and capable, but it is important for a sixteen year old to have someone to be 'around' when your parents can't be, to continue to give support. That is what I would like to do. Like being an aunty.

Abdul: Thank you and you did your best that an aunty even one mom should do.

Emma: Haven't finished yet.

Abdul: I dont know just I am very sad today you know excruciating pain in my heart I want to cry but I dont know I cant I stay in my room it became worse that is why I came here to make my self busy sorry if I toke your time.

Emma: You are not taking my time at all. I cry when I think about what I know that you are going through and I realise there is a lot you have experienced that I do not know. If you don't feel like crying, that is when you are in trouble.

Abdul: Sorry I didnt understand about trouble.

Emma: Like it would be crazy if you didn't cry.

Abdul: yes your right

Emma: I wonder if it is sad for you if I tell you what is happening out here . . . or will it be a distraction?

(Abdul has gone offline)

Emma: I hope you are okay, Abdul. Please keep holding on. I really think we have a chance. We have the computer in our kitchen. And any time you can see that I am on the web please message me. Later let us discuss about telephone contact? It is harder than face-to-face with language, but I am okay if you are?

Abdul told me much later that my belief in him comforted him, and even though he never thought he would ever be allowed to live with us, he didn't want to let me down. He was certain the centre was planning to transfer him to Nauru just like all his friends on Christmas Island had been.

At the same time Abdul was writing to me he was keeping a diary in English. The diary quotes that he has allowed me to include here show just how hard he was trying to learn

43

our language and to stay afloat. This entry reveals his state of mind and what he was hiding—or protecting me from.

ABDUL'S DIARY (undated)

I was in my thought. I thought about the people who died and who killed by other or Taliban and I told to myself what do you want. I thought one day I will die like them, doesn't matter if I am big, small, rich, poor. However you will die one day and doesn't matter today or tomorrow if you couldn't do anything . . . but want do you want to do? Do you want to be a sponger guy? You want to spend your whole life for nothing? Does 'nothing' have the worth to live?

Monday when I wake up I went to wash my face usually when I am washig my face in front of the mirror I am speaking with my self not physical but in my mind and I ask my self that Who are you? What are you? Why are you here? What do you want and why? Then I wash my face and I prayed and I had breakfast and after that again I thought I told my self you want to do so many thing but you can't do anything in here I got really sad then I wrote a request 'Please, please send me to Nauru or Manus Please don't reject please' and I give it to my case manager.

Maybe if I go there I will not have a wish anymore and I never have a dream. I thought with my self, it was much better if I died before in the bomb explosion . . . it was much better that I drowned . . . I die once . . . but now every day I am dieing

(The bomb explosion he refers to was one where he narrowly escaped being blown up in a terrorist attack in Kabul in December 2011.)

There were some indications to me that things were wrong. On Facebook, Abdul told me about Nowruz, the Persian New Year, and an eagerly awaited celebration, but this year without his family and community he would be all alone.

> Sorry yesterday I coudnt chat because yesterday was the first day of the new years in my country and I celeberate with my self in the room I even dont know what will happen with me you know every body is starting thier new years with party and being together but I started with my self and crying I am really sorry if I make you sad because I thought if I tell you maybe I will feel better.

Later, he told me he wasn't allowed to join the group celebrating Nowruz in the detention centre because the 'boss' guard told him it was 'for Iranians only'. This is his diary entry on that day:

ABDUL'S DIARY, 21 March 2014
And now everybody they are starting their New Years Eve to gether with a smile but I am starting with crying my tears, thinking, sitting alone and wish to die and this is my celebration of new year. and told my self the time that I clean my tears. Happy new years Abdul. Happy New year. and after that I cry until about 2.15 a.m. until I sleep.

Chapter 9

A LETTER TO SCOTT MORRISON

The Honourable Mr Scott Morrison
Minister for Immigration
Saturday, 15 March 2014

Dear Mr Morrison,

*Re: Special consideration for unaccompanied minor asylum
seeker, Abdul, boat number HYN071, detained at Blaydin
Point NT since August 2013.*

As Coalition Senator Sue Boyce described, 'In the world
of refugees, there are many deserving causes, but perhaps
none more than that of the Hazara people of Afghanistan,
who, through no fault of their own, survive persecution to

become refugees . . . the plight of the Hazara people is one of the worst.'

We would like to apply for special ministerial consideration and compassion for Abdul's case. We are very happy to work with immigration and propose:

1. making our home an alternative place of detention (APOD) whilst Abdul's case is being decided, or
2. to have his case reviewed as a 'complex case' and to have a decision on his refugee status and be settled with us in Australia as soon as possible.

We would like to have this kept as quiet as possible, and particularly want to avoid having Abdul in the spotlight at all.

Abdul is a sixteen-year-old ethnic Hazara boy who escaped Afghanistan on his own. He is now an unaccompanied minor asylum seeker. He is currently detained at Blaydin APOD in Darwin with orthopaedic and psychiatric medical difficulties. I understand he has been in detention now since August 2013 with no resolution and not surprisingly his mental condition is deteriorating. There is no doubt that he has witnessed horrific events and he was in risk of his life staying in Afghanistan.

His education in Afghanistan had been severely limited by it being too unsafe for him to travel to school. His aims now are to study hard and learn. In the six months since arriving in Australian custody, he has learned English (and other languages) well enough to the extent Serco were using him as a translator. He is clearly a very bright boy with energy and enthusiasm to learn.

Abdul is also a keen athlete. He said he likes to ride bicycles fast (typical teenage boy!), and boxing (although this came with a sad story of trauma for him which indicates the persecution and threat he was personally under, too). I understand that while he has been at Blaydin, his behaviour has been exceptional, and he has undertaken to help other asylum seekers and is helping train a few in basic fitness exercises.

Abdul's main preoccupation when I first met him was that immigration would tell his mother he may have shoulder surgery. He did not want her to worry about him. It is clear that his mum has done a lovely job in parenting this boy, and out of respect for this woman I will never meet I would like to support Abdul. We are not political people and this serves no other purpose but to help this Hazara boy.

I met Abdul when I was visiting Blaydin as an independent medical observer. In that brief meeting, Abdul presented as a very intelligent, caring and earnest teenage boy. He was polite and pleasant, but it was clear that he was not a happy child. The tension in his eyes, although not to the same extent of the thousand-yard stare of the traumatised young mothers in the same camp, is something no one wants to witness in a sixteen year old. At that stage, he had only been detained for four and a half months. There is incontrovertible evidence that the longer children are kept detained like this, the more their mental state weakens and deteriorates.

Over the last few months, Abdul is clearly becoming more despondent and depressed, although he is trying hard to distract himself with school and training. If he goes offshore he will not have this safety net. Despite his severe ordeal, he retains grace and dignity and is a lovely, lovely boy.

Who are we? I am a psychiatrist and my husband, Robert, is a doctor too. We have three boys ages fourteen, eleven and ten. We live in a big house, we have plenty of financial and community support here in Canberra. We have a large stock of 'community capital'. We could have Abdul access good medical care (particularly for his post-traumatic stress disorder), physiotherapy, education and sporting opportunities. We would like Abdul to have the same opportunities for further education and care as our boys do, and we are willing and prepared to foot the bill. This will be a massive cost saving for the government, compared to his being on Christmas Island or Nauru.

We will be able to get him speedy access to expert medical and physiotherapist treatment for his chronically dislocated shoulder. He also requires dental treatment to treat painful teeth due to bruxism, a classic symptom of intense stress. All the available medical literature suggests that his mental health issues are only going to worsen the longer he is in detention, in Australia or offshore. The best chance for his mental health long term is if he resides in the community. We will also get him access to expert mental health treatment.

Our boys and ourselves are aware of the adjustments that will have to be made in our household. They are on board and want to welcome him. Please see their letters. Abdul has a brother in Brisbane. Family connection is important and we would do all we can to support their regular contact.

The wider Canberra community has already offered their support. There has been interest from Anglican and Catholic private schools, the Canberra Medical community, from the local Hazara community, and many others as included in the appendix.

We are also aware that our fitness to look after a sixteen-year-old boy with complex needs will need to be assessed, and we are more than happy for this to happen, and to have regular inspections.

The Royal Australian and New Zealand College of Psychiatrists, the Royal College of Physicians and the Australian Medical association (Position Statements attached in the appendix [to this letter]) are unanimous and have irrefutable evidence that prolonged detention for asylum seekers is harmful to mental health.

Prolonged detention of unaccompanied minors such as Abdul (perhaps inadvertently) violates the following articles of the Convention on the Rights of the Child, to which Australia is a signatory. Article 3, 'In all actions concerning children . . . the best interests of the child shall be a primary consideration'; Article 22, 'A child who is seeking refugee status . . . whether unaccompanied or accompanied . . . [shall] receive appropriate protection and humanitarian assistance'; Article 39, Children subjected to abuse, torture, or armed conflicts should recover 'in an environment which fosters the health, self-respect and dignity of the child'; and Article 37, 'No child shall be deprived of his or her liberty unlawfully or arbitrarily. The arrest, detention or imprisonment of a child shall be in conformity with the law and shall be used only as a measure of last resort and for the shortest appropriate period of time.'

We understand that the government is dealing with a very complex and difficult situation. Abdul is one child. To us, he is a very special person. We are prepared to work with immigration in helping him out of his current dire predicament. And prepared to do this quietly working with immigration as our only concern is Abdul's welfare.

Dr Emma Adams
Psychiatrist
MBBS MMH(Perinat&Inf) FRANZCP

Chapter 10

THE INVISIBLE THREAT

The 'getting Abdul out' year of 2014 was busy. It wasn't long before I had made Wednesdays my Abdul Day, taking this day off work in order to write, lobby and meet with all the people I thought could be helpful in our attempt to get him out of the detention centre.

Not only was I learning the politics of immigration deten-tion and the history of Afghanistan, I was also on a steep learning curve on how to lobby. Many of my friends did not know that people, including children, were being locked away in immigration detention centres again. Once I told them what was happening and what I'd seen, there were often tears for those incarcerated and anger that this was being done in the name of Australia.

Sometimes there were other responses. One woman I knew was adamant that these kids in detention were the 'bad ones', because why else would they be locked up? I had a male acquaintance warn me about having a Muslim in our house. He did not say specifically why this would be a problem, but it was clear this echoed the increasingly racist sentiment capturing our country. One man, who I had known for many years, declined to help in our application because he could not trust my parenting enough to say I was safe for a refugee kid. This was communicated in a snide 'gotcha' way that took me by surprise, but then I realised he was happier to have Abdul and all the other vulnerable kids sent to Nauru on their own.

Many people were reluctant to have their signature on the government record. On the other hand, many of my friends wrote directly to Abdul, wanting to give him more hope and support.

Around this time, I came across an old newspaper article written by Liberal senator Sue Boyce, who while in opposition appeared to be sympathetic to the Hazaras seeking refuge in Australia. On 20 March 2013, she wrote in *The Australian*:

> We supposedly take the issue of human rights seriously and
> so we should; but are these just words confounded by our
> lack of action? What are we saying to these people; getting
> on a leaky boat is worse than genocide?

I quoted from her article in my letter to Scott Morrison and I thought it might be worth approaching her. On contacting Boyce's office, her chief-of-staff suggested I engage a migration agent. He knew that Abdul had arrived after the cut-off date of 19 July 2013, which meant residence was never to be granted, but the chief-of-staff thought that if we could apply for what was known as a Bridging E (class WE) visa, a temporary visa allowing a person to stay in Australia while their application for refugee status is being processed, the application could generate further discussion in the immigration department and help our case. The complexities of the system and the language were mind-boggling. He suggested that Senator Boyce could communicate Abdul's situation to the Minister for Immigration, Scott Morrison.

The bridging visa application was difficult. Not least of those difficulties was getting the paperwork to Abdul. I can understand concerns about potentially dangerous items being smuggled into the detention centres, and I can even understand the ban on chewing gum, but it was a mystery to me why so many parcels I sent Abdul containing important paperwork failed to arrive, just as all the parcels with lollies and treats failed to arrive. Eventually I was forced to smuggle the paperwork in by posting it to a volunteer visitor to the centre, who in turn passed it on to Abdul's friends, and I managed to secure the services of a migration agent, Brian Kelleher, who generously accepted Abdul's case pro bono.

On 5 April 2014, I wrote again to Minister for Immigration, Scott Morrison, this time attaching at least 32 letters of support from various doctors, community members, interested organisations and ministers of religion, together with letters from each of my sons requesting special consideration for Abdul and his release into our care:

I, Dr Adams, have come to know Abdul well. He has made
a huge impact on our family's heart [. . .] There is no agenda

apart from our desire to welcome Abdul into our home until he is able to support himself as a well-educated contributing member of society [. . .] The benefit for Abdul will be positive, particularly compared to prolonged detention. The Department will save significant amounts of money. We will make sure that immigration's interest in confidentiality is upheld. Our agenda is Abdul, not politics.

On 6 June 2014, the Secretary of the Department of Immigration, Martin Bowles, acknowledged our 'concern for Master _____ and your very generous and compassionate offer of accommodation and emotional support' but 'at this time the minister has indicated that he is not inclined to exercise either of these public interest options'.

This was a setback and bad news for Abdul. But, doggedly, I pushed back and wrote a reply to Bowles and Morrison.

'We would like to make our position clearer to the Department of Immigration [. . .] We consider Abdul a part of our family. We don't just give up on family. We will be watching closely what happens to Abdul, along with our large network and support base.'

Over the following months, I wrote scores of letters and emails pleading Abdul's case to Minister Morrison and his advisors. As Abdul's mental health deteriorated, I also wrote to IHMS and Serco. My initial letters had tried to appeal to the minister's sense of kindness, common sense and compassion; my subsequent correspondence appealed to financial savings for immigration if our family looked after Abdul. The only alternatives given by immigration were further detention in either Darwin or Nauru with no end in sight, or back to Afghanistan.

Chapter 11

LETTERS FROM MY SONS

Honourable Mr Scott Morrison
Minister for Immigration
Wednesday, 19 March 2014

Dear Mr Minister,

My parents want to bring Abdul to live with us. Abdul is only seventeen months older than me, but for the last eight months he has been locked up and before that he had been living in fear of his life because he is a Hazara from Afghanistan.

If he lives with us, some advantages would be that he is out of the detention centre. Some advantages to us would be that we know it is the right thing to do. My mum has met him and says he is a nice kid, and we can learn a lot from him.

There could be some disadvantages, including the house being more crowded, but this is not a big issue for us because we have plenty of room; we even have a bedroom ready for him. Another issue is communication if his English isn't very good, but he is learning very quickly; even quicker if he comes to live with us. Mum says he is very keen on studying and going to school so I suppose he is going to learn quickly.

We have a lot of support from family and friends who know about Abdul and who will help us help him. We are also going to learn to speak some Hazaragi from the Hazara community in Canberra when we know he's coming as they will help us and Abdul too.

I humbly request you to please give special consideration for Abdul as he is a special case and our family is really well set up for him, and I want him to stay with us.

Yours sincerely,

Jasper
Age 14

Honourable Mr Scott Morrison
Minister for Immigration
Saturday, 15 March 2014

Dear Mr Minister,

My mum and dad have been talking about fostering an asylum
seeker named Abdul. He is sixteen years old and alone in
Australia because he escaped from Afghanistan.

When he comes, lots of things in my life will change, such
as the house will be more crowded and my younger brother
gets the upstairs room, which bugs me. Mum says there might
be a few problems to start, but that Dad and Mum will always
work things out for me.

But there will also be some very good things. We will
learn about other places in the world, and we are doing a
good thing.

Father Richard at my school says I should include him in my
prayers. Many of our friends also think this is a good thing we
are doing.

Please let Abdul come and stay with us, he sounds really
cool and he cares about us too.

Yours sincerely

Lucas
Age 11

Letters from my sons

Honourable Mr Scott Morrison
Minister for Immigration
Saturday, 15 March 2014

Dear Mr Minister,

My mum and dad have been talking about having Abdul to
come and live here with us. Abdul is a nice kid and I want him
to live with us too so that:

1. He will be free :)
2. When my dad buys a pack of six hamburger rolls there
   will not be one left over
3. I will have another big brother to do stuff with!!
4. We can teach him how to be an Australian!
5. It's the right thing to do

We have a room ready for him and we want him to come.
My mum says we can have doctors for him as well!

Please let him come to us.

Yours sincerely

Toby
Age 10, class 5EP

Chapter 12

THE BACK-UP PLAN

I had met Abdul in early summer and it was now winter. The single-handed campaigning, the late nights messaging Abdul and my worry about him had been going on for many months. As a family, we would walk in the bush together on the weekends, the boys trying to collect the biggest cow bones they could find, and we'd cook sausages over a wood fire. Jasper's quiet philosophical comments on life, or Lucas and Toby playing the clown together in their last flash of kid-ness before teenagehood arrived, were an antidote to my preoccupations. Rob took up a new hobby of baking bread, and when I took my weekly long runs, which restored my equanimity, he would keep me company on his bike. Worried but undeterred by the replies I had received from immigration, I decided I needed a back-up plan in case the worst happened and they decided to send Abdul to Nauru or even Afghanistan. I wanted to create a network of people in the public arena—not just our acquaintances—who would know about Abdul so that if something happened to him it would not happen in silence.

I spoke with one of the organisers of the Canberra Refugee Action Committee. He challenged my idealism, explaining that most Australians didn't care about people in detention and that requesting kindness for this one asylum seeker was unlikely to gain any traction. He pointed out that polling in 2013 showed that about 60 per cent of people thought most boat arrivals were not genuine refugees despite the 90–95 per cent who were proven to be just that. The poll also indicated that 60 per cent of Australians thought asylum seekers should be treated more harshly.

While these statistics depressed me, the many other caring Australians I met along the way buoyed my spirits. One of these people was Professor William Maley, one of Australia's leading academic experts on Afghanistan, whose unruffled and cultured manner contrasted with the horrific stories he told me about the situation there. His kindness extended to later providing his expert opinion in our application—which he had already given to government agencies—on the danger to Hazaras of returning to Afghanistan. While I will always be grateful for his time, reading Professor Maley's work, which documented attacks and bombings, the difficulties of returned people finding any way of supporting themselves and the vulnerability that young returnees have to sexual exploitation, only led to more sleepless nights.

I sat with Father Nikolai Blaskow, an Anglican minister, as I told him my story in the calm space of the chapel. I needed his perspective and advice, as he had been a child refugee himself. When I'd finished talking with this kind and generous man, he offered prayers for my family and for Abdul, and he said he was happy to support us with a letter. He also offered to introduce me to church leaders of other denominations.

The ministers, priests and nuns I spoke with walked their talk. I saw them at rallies defending human rights, and in the community running programs to help refugees and asylum seekers. They were all happy to encourage and assist us in our efforts for Abdul. Father Blaskow's prayers, and the goodness and charity of these Christians, gave me the courage and fortitude I needed to go on. But that was not their only gift. As a lifelong atheist, I used to think that prayers were useless things, yet in this long journey their prayers have fostered a connection in me with something greater.

At a rally, I was introduced to barrister and human rights advocate Julian Burnside. I told him about my endeavour to help Abdul. When I heard he was heading to Darwin, I asked if he might meet him, hoping he could be another of the 'witnesses' I was gathering on Abdul's behalf. He said he would try his best, but probably wouldn't have time.

Maybe it was the hand of some god, but Julian Burnside's return flight from Darwin was delayed by ash from a volcanic eruption in Bali and the chance to meet Abdul presented itself. When they met, Mr Burnside tempered Abdul's expectations about the chances of us getting him out, while at the same time explaining his efforts to improve conditions inside the detention centres.

Mostly, for Abdul and me, the support was what mattered—knowing that people knew and cared. But there were days when even that didn't feel like enough.

Abdul: actually I want to know many thing I want to know about my self that who I am and why sometime I am feeling to call my mom that your son need you I cant do it any more without you its very hard.

Emma: It is so hard. When I think about my own sons in your position it is too upsetting. But what does your mother want for you? Mums want the best for their kids.

Abdul: she did what she could for me but what about me she is still the same situation but I cant do any thing for her.

Chapter 13

THE SECOND VISIT

I was not able to see Abdul again until August 2014, nine months after we had first met.

A visit to the Darwin detention centres from Canberra was not an easy venture. First, I had to ask permission from Serco, which required many emails and forms. Visiting hours were restricted and so I had to plan the trip with precision to maximise my time with Abdul. It takes about six hours to fly from Canberra to Darwin, but with stopovers in Sydney or Adelaide, along with the time it takes to get a rental car and drive to the Blaydin detention centre at Wickham Point, it took a whole day to get there. If I left Canberra at 6 a.m. and everything went to plan, I could manage to get to the detention centre at 5 p.m.

I took along a picnic feast of carefully packed Afghan

food, hoping it would help allay Abdul's homesickness. The only Afghan restaurant in Canberra had closed down, but I found the owners and discovered they were now running a pizza shop. When they knew why I wanted Afghan food, the owner asked his mum to cook up a lovely selection of *bolani* (a fried pocket bread filled with pumpkin and potato), *mantoo* (steamed ravioli parcels filled with spiced meat) and *kabuli pilau*, pressure-cooked fatty meat on a bed of spiced rice with cardamom and carrots. It smelled delicious and I knew that it was made with love for this unknown child.

I arrived at Wickham Point and Blaydin APOD at sunset. I handed in my phone and had my bags searched. Luckily the Serco guards allowed me to bring the hamper of food in. I was escorted to the meeting room and was left there while Abdul was summoned.

The room smelt stale and there were dirty cups and plates piled up on the sink. While I waited, I washed up and cleared the garbage. I wanted the place to look nice for our short visit. As I didn't want the guard eavesdropping on our conversation, I set out our Afghan feast on the outside table, braving the mosquitos and the humid evening for some privacy.

It was only when Abdul arrived that I understood the immensity of my relief. He was there in front of me, he had not given up, and the reality that this person I had become attached to was still in this horrid place hit home. When we hugged—kind of awkwardly—my tears burst out despite me trying to hold them back. It had been a long day with two take-offs and two landings, and although I am a frequent flyer

I am also a nervous one. It had been all a bit too much. Along with the car hire, the drive and checking in to the detention centre, there was being away from my boys and the cancelling of patients . . . Was it perhaps a little crazy to do all this for a stranger? But that hug—that human connection from a kid who needed a hug just like my sons—reassured me that I had done the right thing.

We talked about his family in Afghanistan, his mother and all of his siblings still there, and about his brother Ahad, who also arrived in Australia as an unaccompanied minor before him. They had not seen each other for three years. This was the first chance we had to talk freely so we talked and talked until I was told by the guards it was time to go and I realised that we never even looked at the food.

After about the fifth reminder to leave, I left Abdul and walked back out into the quiet. Inside the fence, Blaydin reeks of despair, while outside is a forbidding landscape. Past the silhouettes of the gnarled eucalypts in the deep, eerie darkness were the mangroves, with their familiar swampy smell of saltwater and mud. I was glad to hear the crunch of the dirt road under my feet. Back in my hotel room in Darwin that night, I sat awake, wretched, until the early hours of the morning.

✕✕✕✕✕✕✕

The next day, before the centre opened for visitors, I visited the Parap markets to have coffee with Georgie and later Justine, two women I'd made contact with during my first visit to Darwin. These women had known Abdul and many others in the centres through their efforts to advocate for the detained asylum seekers. I will be eternally grateful for the comfort and especially the courage they gave me that morning, because I knew that at the end of my short visit to Blaydin I would have to say goodbye to Abdul and I was dreading it.

Abdul spent the morning telling me about his home, the mountains in Afghanistan and the valleys full of apple trees, while I told him about the Australian bush, its birds and animals, and how it can vary so much from desert to gentle farmland to rainforest. Despite our distracting conversations, leaving was as bad as I expected. Abdul smiled the whole time; I don't know how he did it. Leaving this boy alone in that place while I walked away ripped my heart out. On the drive back to Darwin Airport I had to pull over twice to wipe my eyes and pull myself together. Why do tears come so easily in airports and planes? Maybe it's the accumulated separations in these places that have left an imprint. On the four-hour flight to Adelaide, it was difficult to hide my tears.

As I waited for my connecting flight to Canberra, I took myself off for a solid meal, a glass of wine and a phone call to Rob. I wanted to hear my husband's calm voice. I thought this reassuring contact would keep me together until I got home. I described what a horrible place it was, and when Rob asked how Abdul was I burst into tears again.

I had to cancel my patients for the following day as I didn't think it would be a good look professionally to be weeping at the drop of a hat. It was my first sick day for about fifteen years.

For the rest of that week, the hundreds of sandfly bites I'd got in Blaydin kept me awake and itching each night, while the pain in my chest from my ripped-apart heart would not leave.

> Out
> Of a great need
> We are all holding hands
> And climbing.
> Not loving is a letting go.
> Listen,
> The terrain around here
> Is far too dangerous for that.

> —Hafiz

Chapter 14

DESPAIR

As 2014 dragged on, and Abdul's mental state continued to deteriorate, it was suggested to me that I had been too naive in appealing to kindness in communicating with the immigration department. Instead the focus should have been on Abdul's safety and the risk to immigration's reputation if anything happened to him.

I had deliberately avoided this approach because I hadn't wanted to be too pushy with my credentials as a psychiatrist. As Abdul's case stalled, it became clear that my approach needed to change: to help Abdul I *needed* to be pushy. I was also reminded to challenge my trepidation when a strong and experienced woman reassured me, 'Public servants are your servants. You pay them and they work for you!'

Embracing this new strategy, my letters changed, leaving the Department of Immigration in no doubt that, as a psychiatrist, I understood that Abdul was unwell. In fact, he was a suicide risk, along with many other people in the facility. This meant there would be enormous legalities, paperwork and publicity for the department if something happened to Abdul after they had been informed of this risk. I subsequently learned that they had been repeatedly informed of the same risk to Abdul from the many other health professionals employed at the centre during that year.

Abdul could no longer hide the flatness in his voice in our rare telephone conversations. There was a hopelessness and helplessness that had not been there before. His Facebook posts described the inevitability of death and I was scared he was breaking. When weeks passed and I did not hear from him, I feared that he had given up, or that he had already been taken away to another facility.

My dear Abdul knows this a hundred times more than me: one of the most terrible experiences in the world is to witness a loved one being harmed and not being able to do anything to help them. I felt useless and guilty that perhaps I had offered false hope to this vulnerable boy.

I had one tangible thread of our connection—a barely identifiable photo of Abdul I had found on Facebook. I put this photo in the kitchen, stuck on a cabinet behind our dinner table, so I could imagine Abdul being with us during meals. I needed his image to stay strong.

Soon after I had started communicating with Abdul, I connected with his brother Ahad on Facebook, and then phoned him, telling him of my plans and hoping that he would be an ally in getting Abdul out of detention. He was surprised that I would want to do this, but he was positive and said he would support my efforts in whatever way he could. I kept in contact with Ahad, especially as we were both worried about Abdul's wellbeing. I also found out about some other relatives living in Brisbane and contacted them to tell them of my plan, despite their inability to assist, as this was the proper thing to do.

In between all of this, Rob and our boys needed to live their own lives. My boys also needed their mother and I needed to be present for them. Then there were the day-to-day parenting tasks: making sure teeth were brushed and kids were bathed regularly; sorting out skirmishes between brothers; cooking enormous amounts of food; getting them to music concerts; sports training; parent–teacher meetings; having their friends over; and the whole, busy life of home. Jasper had taken to making water rockets, meaning Rob and my alertness levels were increased after he and his mates were found climbing up trees to dizzying heights in order to retrieve their equipment. Lucas was focused on his music and we were mindful of monitoring his time on computer games, while Toby was making plans for earning money to buy a remote-controlled drone with virtual goggles so he could experience the thrill of flying. On top of all this, I had my marriage to look after and a practice to run.

Every day I followed the news and began to know when Parliament was sitting and when bills relating to children in detention were to be debated. On an intellectual level,

I learned about the machinations of our parliamentary system. On an emotional level, it was devastating to see the heartlessness of politicians in both major political parties. They had inured themselves to the suffering of these people and the breaking of Australia's international legal obligations.

I also followed the news from Afghanistan as best I could, in an effort to understand the place Abdul came from. The country has been war-torn for almost 40 years, but because there is limited news coverage of Afghanistan in Australia we are not always aware of the magnitude of the terror and bloodshed, which can make it hard for Australians to fully understand why people are fleeing. Unlike us in the West, Afghans constantly experience the horrors of war in their lives and in their newsfeeds. Searching international news broadcasts, week after week, I would come across pictures of murdered children and mutilated bodies amid evidence of the ongoing chaos, and I came to understand that this is Afghanistan's reality—and Abdul had lived it.

Back at home, I felt like I was holding my breath, wondering about this fourth boy who I was failing to help and who I had not heard from. And then, after weeks of silence, Abdul called. That he wanted to talk, and wanted me to know he was alright, gave me hope again.

'Your job is to stay safe, stay polite and quiet,' I told him. 'Hold on. Please do not give in to despair.'

And yet the despair sometimes threatened to drown me too. My anxiety and anguish took such a toll on me that I sometimes wondered what I had left in myself to keep going.

Chapter 15

BIRDS

When I was a curious three year old, with golden brown hair falling in ringlets over my shoulders (until I played with scissors and cut them off), another little girl across the street told me that people took pills to make themselves better. I knew there were pills at home so I pulled a chair into the bathroom, climbed onto the sink and reached up on tippy-toes until I felt the metal box of bright-red tablets. Then I ate them.

A few minutes later I felt very sick and very scared. My skin burned and everything was so bright it hurt my eyes. Worse still, the little dogs on my pyjamas were biting me. The ambulance people were the blue and pink monsters from *Sesame Street* and they held me down so I couldn't breathe. I screamed when they drove me away from my mum and dad.

When my family recalls this story they laugh, because I was so naughty and that night I also bit a nurse. What I remember, though, is terror and feeling trapped.

Much of my childhood was full of happiness and exploration. My first solo expedition was when I was five; I hauled my supplies—a shirt and a blanket, apples, cheese and some bandaids—in a toy cart into the mangrove swamps along the Georges River in Sydney. But the best adventures in the bush were always with my gran.

Gran took the 'interesting' routes, including squeezing us into the 'bat cave'—a small, hidden crack high up in the amphitheatre of a sandstone cliff—until we were surrounded by the lovely stink of guano and dozens of flapping bats. We always took our time on the walks: finding flannel flowers on a bright spring day, looking for cherry ballarts and maybe having a taste of the tart, sweet double berries.

Along the way, Gran would tell me happy stories, but also stories of how her mother wasn't free as a child: how she was a servant to her supposed 'foster' mother who scrubbed her brown skin raw. I knew the stories were sad, but I was too small to understand what she was telling me. Remembering those days in the bush, with the shimmering sky seen through a net of gum leaves and the sparkle of sun on the saltwater Georges River, never fails to lift my spirits.

Another secret of my childhood was that I could fly. As a bigger kid, I would tie the corners of a sheet to my wrists, climb onto the steep pitch of the roof and jump. The feeling of falling, and my ability to land and roll, was exhilarating, but

I never seemed to be able to skim along the ground and soar back up into the air as I imagined I should.

Watching birds fly and imagining that freedom always fascinated me. Perhaps that is why I had a box, lovingly lined with cottonwool, ready for a rescue mission if any baby bird fell out of its nest. I wanted to feel a grateful, fluffy little bird in my hands. Perhaps we could be friends and we could have adventures together?

When I finally found one, the reality was not as pretty as I had imagined. Baby birds are raw-skinned, pot-bellied creatures with scrawny necks and bulgy eyes. This one opened its mouth a lot, but did not make any sound. It refused to thrive despite all the care I gave it. This was a crisis for a nine-year-old. Was I helping my bird by feeding her or was I prolonging her agony? Then the scent of death took over and there was nothing more I could do.

Months after the bird died, my father brought home a baby possum that had fallen from his mother's pouch. Possum was another pink, fragile creature that looked just like the sheep and dog embryos my father, who was a vet, kept in formaldehyde bottles on our mantelpiece. We tried so hard to save him, but he died in a pool of diarrhoea.

Perhaps my parents thought these experiences were too unsettling, as the next animals that came home were two poddy lambs. My sisters and I would sing to them, 'Wham, Bam, I am a Lamb!'—this was the 1980s and George Michael was fab. The sturdy lambs would butt their heads against our legs and they suckled milk so hard from the rubber-glove teated beer bottles we had to hold on with two hands.

The lambs grew up and were returned to the farm where I was told they had a long and fruitful life forever after.

Alongside the glorious freedom of a childhood outdoors was the terrifying ordeal of asthma. Especially frightening were those episodes in the coldest part of the night when I woke up alone, wheezing, coughing and struggling for breath. When breathing became exhausting, even at that age, I saw the signposts to death.

In the early days, there weren't many medicines to manage asthma well. There was a powder that made my throat itchy and raspy, and a foul yellow syrup that tasted like a punishment. There was another syrup that was better because it reminded me of lemonade, but it made my heart flutter and my arms and legs go weak and jittery. My mother was told to percuss, which meant draping me across her knees and thumping my back several times a day, but this hurt a lot and felt like even more punishment. It also did nothing for my chest.

One day I had an asthma attack at a school sports carnival and was taken to the hospital. I don't remember much about it, except for the cold sheet of the bed and being too scared to lie down because my chest was struggling to move. A mask, with pulsating white mist, was lowered over my nose and mouth, and I wanted to rip it off. My face became wet and chilly, then, slowly but surely, my chest loosened and I could breathe again: a magical feeling of lightness, silver clarity and freedom.

Once my asthma was under control, my confidence returned. I spent many hours of my teenage years riding a bicycle through the countryside of Armidale in New South Wales where my family had moved for my father's work. Any day not at school I would be on my bike, ending up in the towns of Uralla, Guyra or Hillgrove, or cycling to the gorge country where the land tipped into ravines and huge waterfalls tumbled over the sharp edges. The change of seasons provided its own adventure. I loved the white-frosted winter wonderland, the first pink plum blossoms in spring and the green grassy paddocks dotted with big white daisies in summer.

Cycling gave me freedom. Using my strength and lungs and heart to travel, I connected with the hills and the landscape, always in control of where I wanted to go. Nowadays, running gives me that freedom. Running sustains me: there is certainty in running. If I want to run up a mountain, and I put in the effort, I get to the top. It's simple and fair. Running— being free and in control—is the way I reconnect myself to the earth. It is also the way I reconnect to myself.

Perhaps all of this is what I saw in Abdul. Perhaps I recognised his intrepid heart and his need to be free. I hated that he was locked up in that horrible place and that his freedom had been stolen. In my own small way, I knew a little of what it was like to be trapped and scared.

Chapter 16

THE HAPPIEST KID IN DETENTION

Abdul on Facebook: If all the people live together happy no more war just love doesnt matter if I stay whole my live in detention centre and I will be more happy then them just to see the other people happy

One day, during a rare conversation on the telephone, Abdul told me that people thought he was the happiest kid in detention. The guards couldn't understand how he, a teenage boy with no family to support him and no hope, could be so happy. I wondered how they could have thought this, until I remembered how they only saw cuteness when they looked at the traumatised baby sitting alone in the sandpit.

All around Abdul, kids were breaking apart. He had to restrain an adolescent friend who had become psychotic and was bashing his bloodied head against the wall. He witnessed a young friend jump off the second-floor roof of the detention centre. Abdul told me that he heard her screaming but by the time he raced over she was already on the ground, her body distorted, and in agony. She was taken to hospital and he heard that afterwards she was moved out of the detention centre and into, I presume, community detention. Abdul didn't know where she was taken and he never saw her again.

His response to the tragedies around him was to form a secret plan: to stay happy and friendly. 'I knew they were all having a bad time there,' he told me. 'If I was depressed, it would make them feel worse, so I wanted to keep some motivation for them.' Of course he wasn't happy, but this pretence was all he could do to keep himself afloat—and, of, course it was his way of raising a middle finger to immigration. He told me that he knew 'they wanted to break me and make me suffer and they aren't going to win'. He hoped that if they saw their efforts were failing then perhaps they would think it wasn't going to work with others. Then, he told me, 'they would stop being so cruel'.

One of the problems for Abdul, as with all the other teenagers in detention, was that there was very little to do. Computer access was limited, excursions outside the centre (escorted by guards) were rare, and there was nowhere to go in the compound. Unlike the other teenagers, though, Abdul didn't have family with him for support. Under these conditions, exercise was the only healthy outlet for an adventurous teenage boy.

He tried so hard to be the 'happiest boy' he got shin splints from skipping. There was a swimming pool in one detention compound and Abdul taught himself how to swim by watching videos on the internet. He kept up his swimming even as his damaged shoulder threatened to dislocate. The guards told him to stop exercising because his body was breaking, but no one seemed to consider how his spirit was breaking too. Our internet messages around this time revealed a boy steadily slipping away.

The Minister for Immigration is the legal guardian of children in immigration detention. Thinking about the implications of a politician with his own political motives being responsible for the welfare of these vulnerable children brings to mind the saying about foxes guarding the hen house. However, the day-to-day decisions regarding Abdul's wellbeing were delegated to a public servant.

Even before my second visit I was so desperately worried about Abdul's mental and emotional state that I wrote directly to this Department of Immigration official on 9 July 2014. Stressing my fears for Abdul's wellbeing and my concerns about the increasing damage being done with his continued incarceration, I bluntly reminded him that his responsibility was to the child, not to the political agendas of the minister.

'Do you think it is good enough to sit back and just accept this?' I wrote. 'Can you live with yourself knowing that there was an entirely reasonable option and you did not try to do more?' I never received a reply to my letter, but two weeks later a psychiatrist visited Abdul. A second saw him the following month.

It's possible that my letters, pointing out he was at serious risk, might have helped arrange that first appointment, but it's just as likely that it was because he told the guards he was going to run away. Two Vietnamese boys had recently escaped and were still in hiding. Another escapee would have meant more unwelcome attention for the centre and further bad press for immigration.

Abdul on Facebook: Yep actually I had a joke about run away from detention with the serco then they toke it serious and I told them that if I want to run a way no body can stop me because this is what make me different from others and if I decide to do some thing I will do it no matter how dangrous and how difficult it is. Hahaha!

Emma: Oh Abdul, be careful!

Abdul: It was a silly joke.

Emma: It probably freaked them out! My job is to make them feel uncomfortable with you in detention and I'd prefer to have you safe and sound with us. But let's see if we can play by the rules.

Abdul: Lets see, trying different thing.

Later, we would obtain Abdul's medical files under the Freedom of Information Act. The following excerpts are included with Abdul's full permission, which is an act of bravery. The medical notes describe a young man with significant mental health problems, including post-traumatic stress disorder (PTSD), anxiety and depression. The psychiatrist described Abdul as a:

> somewhat sad-looking lad, good rapport, cooperative, appropriate answers to questions, reasonable eye contact . . . Seen with interpreter but Abdul communicating most of the session in English . . . Mood depression greater than 10/10 bad and significant anxiety, affect flat, quite sad at times.

He noted that Abdul:

> describes his mood as very sad, 'everyone in here is depressed'. States depression is greater than 10/10 bad, can sometimes go for days. Sometimes feels better for a few hours after a sleep but will then move back again into depression . . . Sleep a major problem, awake all night, sleeps 5 a.m. to 11 a.m. Reads and writes at night, often struggles with negative and worrying thoughts.

Abdul also had the full-hand of classic symptoms of PTSD:

> Can become very anxious when thinking of traumas from the past. Describes witnessing much suffering, killing, explosions, these coming back into his mind usually when sleeping. Physiological triggering when these happen with his body shaking, face flushing, shortness of breath.

Describes this happening in Afghanistan a lot. Can happen here 3–4 times a week.

Does get triggered into anxiety and somatic symptoms e.g. even with a small argument between people here in the centre. Will get triggered by movies with violence, tends to avoid these. An action movie will move him into body shaking, upset, headaches. Nightmares of the incidents when sleeping. Describes somatic feeling of someone smothering him at night a few weeks ago.

The psychiatrist elsewhere recorded:

Does feel at times he would be better off dead, feels 'there is no other way', but would not kill himself because of family and religion.

Around this time, Abdul would write in his diary:

It was about 3 a.m. in the middle of the night, I had a very bad dream that there was so many people in my room and they try to hurt me but I couldnt shout, I couldnt move. Then once I wake up and I shout . . . I felt that all my body is lock . . . When I woke up there wasn't any one but still I could hear the sound of them. Then I put three blanket on my self to avoid the sound. But it doesn't work and I didnt sleep until morning.

In late August 2014, when I had not heard anything from Abdul for ten days, I was worried. I rang Abdul's friend Georgie, who had previously been his teacher in Darwin and now was a visitor at the detention centre. She told me that Abdul was not in a good way and had punched a mirror in his room.

When I later read Abdul's file, I discovered that he was seeing mental health workers whose focus was assessment for self-harm or harm to others. Most of the appointments did not have a diagnosis or indicate any specific treatment, although one psychiatric nurse suggested that Abdul have cognitive behavioural therapy to change 'his negative attitude'. What was particularly painful for me to read in these documents was the way one psychologist repeatedly referred to Abdul in her counselling notes as 'HYN071'. Apparently Abdul didn't even warrant a name.

As a health care professional, I've often wondered how a young boy could be referred to as mere letters and numbers, and why the clear-cut signs of his mental illness were sometimes not even seen. Perhaps people who have worked in the detention centres for too long, and have become so accustomed or so numbed by suffering, can no longer see it for what it is? Maybe just to survive in the system they have developed a wilful blindness or a type of dissociation? It appears to me that everyone in the centres—including the health staff and guards—are at risk of their own mental health issues affecting their judgement. This, along with what seems to be inadequate basic mental health knowledge, training and support means that life in detention remains unsafe for those who are mentally unwell.

One can only hope that any psychiatrist working in these detention centres has a genuine desire to make a bad situation better. And yet they must know that their recommendations are often ignored. If that is the case, then I suggest that they are treading a thin ethical line. The doctors' presence alone has been used as an argument that appropriate care has been given. This could be interpreted as complicity.

Not only do the doctors who work in detention centres face loyalty conflicts between the interests of their employer and the best interests of their patients, they face interference from government into their clinical management. They can never be entirely sure what non-medical purpose their notes may be used for and they can never assure patient confidentiality. Until recently, doctors faced prison if they inadvertently disclosed information about conditions in the detention centres or if they advocated for children facing abuse, including sexual abuse in offshore centres, under the *Australian Border Force Act 2015*.

These doctors also work in the knowledge that the best care they can provide will almost always be deficient. Paid handsomely by IHMS, they are faced with a senseless and unending task because no one's mental health gets better in detention. The evidence, including data collected by the IHMS health service itself, indicates that the longer people are held in detention, the worse they get. The detention centres have been rightly called 'factories for mental illness' by distinguished psychiatrist and Australian of the Year, Professor Patrick McGorry AO. Dr Peter Young, former director of mental health services for IHMS and now whistle-blower, described the indefinite incarceration of asylum seekers as 'torture', and Professor Louise Newman, the psychiatrist in the independent immigration health advisory group disbanded by the new government in 2013, said the policy was 'inhumane' and 'wilfully and deliberately causing harm to adults and children'. I don't think that any doctor truly believes that antidepressant or antipsychotic medications will properly work in such a setting.

In October, Abdul, along with other unaccompanied minors, was taken on an excursion. It was a big occasion for him because this was his first visit to a cinema. Unbelievably, the guards chose *Fury* for these traumatised teenagers, one of the most distressing war movies imaginable. Lauded for its realism, the film has intensely graphic scenes of explosions, shooting deaths, soldiers killing children, people having their throats slit and being crushed by tanks, decapitation and rape. To this day, I wonder if this was an act of deliberate spite by the guards or just plain stupidity. Or was it simply them not giving a shit about the children in their care?

As could be expected, the movie reignited Abdul's trauma and affected him so badly that he couldn't go to school the following day.

All this is not to say that Abdul had no support in detention. There were many health staff and many guards who were very kind to Abdul. But while they could soothe him in the moment, they could do nothing to change his situation or to prevent his decline.

With his mental state disintegrating, Abdul disclosed to a second psychiatrist what he had also written in his diary, that he was hearing a voice telling him he was no good and that they were coming to get him. He also had a bodily feeling one night of someone smothering him. Hearing voices does not necessarily mean psychosis or schizophrenia, but all were signs that Abdul's abnormally strong coping system was deteriorating. They were not signs of weakness but of damage that could have been repaired with removal from detention and good clinical care.

Each time the psychiatrists saw him they recommended Abdul as a 'very strong candidate for community detention'. One doctor wrote:

> The fact he is in the detention centre on his own with no family supports at his age and struggling with significant PTSD symptoms, as well as significant physical health problems, leaves him at risk of developing entrenched mental health problems. Ongoing counselling will obviously help with this but is not going to be enough with the complex mixture of issues and a lack of support for him at his age.

It was obvious to anyone that this boy should not have been in the centre, but still the recommendation to move him was ignored.

Chapter 17

THE THIRD VISIT

I was so worried about Abdul that I travelled to Darwin in September 2014, only six weeks after my previous visit. Despite my pressing need to see Abdul, I was dreading the return to the Northern Territory. The bumpy plane descent, the heat, and the detention centre itself intimidated me. I was also afraid of what I might find there.

As soon as the plane landed, I rushed to the detention centre, arriving at 4 p.m., but I had to wait outside the visitor centre at the mercy of swarms of sandflies until the guards let me in. I heard the school bus arrive back at the centre a bit after 4.15, and through the wooden slats of the fence I could see a white minivan full of teenagers pull up. I knew that Abdul was one of those inside. I heard their yells and cheers, but for another slow twenty minutes the kids had to sit in the bus in the tropical sun. I could hear them calling out, 'Officer! Officer!', wanting to be let back in to the compound. Witnessing yet another example of shoddy care, I felt my frustration and resentment rise, but at the same time the kids' high spirits and cheekiness made me feel proud of them: they were pushing back.

After the guards opened the gate and the van drove through, I waited expectantly. Eventually Abdul walked into the visitors' room. He didn't look so good. I could see none of his usual self-possession, and despite his efforts to be cheerful and entertaining, something was amiss. It hit home how much Abdul had been 'faking it' in our Facebook messages. Clearly he was struggling a lot more than he had let on.

This time, rather than a big meal, I brought along iced tea, biscuits and extra food that Abdul could have later. We sat outside again. At some point Abdul remembered that he wanted to show me his school reports and ran to his room to retrieve them. While he was gone, I moved into the cool meeting room to wait—I needed a reprieve from the sandflies. I also wanted to listen more closely to what was happening inside.

An Iranian man was playing the violin with a group of about eight men and women seated on the couches and on the floor around him. I was mesmerised by this music and the audience were just as entranced; some sighed and others swayed with their eyes closed in appreciation. As the beautiful music washed over us, I felt like we were all some-where else, an elegant salon, not this grimy detention centre full of despairing people.

'That was beautiful,' I said when the playing stopped.

'Thank you,' the man replied in very good English. And then: 'Do you play?'

'Yes, but not like you.' He had been playing Persian music. It was sensual and longing, the melody plaintive, meandering and sinuous with an intense rhythm and pauses like breathing. 'Your music is so different to my ears.'

He pushed the violin into my hands. Despite it being a cheap, mass-produced instrument, it had the piney scent of rosin and wood polish.

'A guard lent me this. I could not take my violin on the boat.' He looked into my eyes. 'You please play too.'

Feeling shy—I had only spoken up to start with because I didn't want the awkwardness of being an eavesdropper—but also knowing that I couldn't hand it back without offering something in return, I turned the pegs to tune the violin to the brighter but harsher Western musical scale. As I tucked the violin under my chin, I could feel the warmth of the man lingering in the instrument. My hands were shaking, and I had to pause, wondering if I could remember anything to play as I hadn't practised properly in almost 30 years. My performance, if it could be called that, was as shabby as I expected, but everyone seemed polite and engaged. Relieved that it was over, I handed the violin back and the man smiled kindly as I apologised for un-tuning it.

What an odd situation, I thought. Why are these talented and sophisticated people locked up in here? What happens to their lives, dreams and talents? And does it matter if a person locked up like this is accomplished or not? Of course it doesn't. The stark inhumanity of this bizarre situation made me feel as if I were in a dream about the end of the world. For me, it was unreality; for them, being trapped there was their stark reality.

By the time Abdul returned, I was feeling overwhelmed, so rather than talk further I thanked everybody for their hospitality and we went outside again. This time the mood between us was even more sombre. With our hope for a speedy resolution to Abdul's incarceration gone, the spark had left his eyes.

Despite my worry, there was nothing more I could do to change the situation. I had repeatedly written to the department, the minister, the psychiatrists and the detention centre. Yet Abdul was still in this place. All that was said was that the centre could increase his supervision. And when Abdul really chose to kill himself (I was not thinking 'if' in that continuing situation but 'when') there would be no way to stop him.

I put my arm around his shoulders and I smelled the top of his head, like I would a baby, a deeply biological instinct. I sat and studied his face in the late twilight, trying to store every detail. I knew I was doing it so I could remember him in case the worst happened. We were not allowed to take photographs in the detention centre and I had only that grainy old picture from Facebook pinned up at home.

The next evening, Abdul was waiting at the gate for me when I arrived, the backdrop of a spectacular Darwin sunset at his back. Although the visiting hours had already started, there were no guards to let me in. What a wonderful opportunity! I took a photograph of him standing on a rock in the compound wearing his school T-shirt and backpack with the pockmarked asphalt and container housing behind him. He tried to be cheerful, but I could see the effort it was taking. He told me he had been on suicide watch recently, and as the tears came down his face he asked me not to cry.

After this visit, I went back to my hotel room and cried. I didn't want to infect Rob and the boys with my melancholy so when I called them I pretended everything was okay. I listened to their stories of the day, which were stable, fun and happy.

That final Saturday morning, I brought fresh fruit and food from the markets to the detention centre, along with as cheerful a face as I could. It wasn't a long visit, and all I could do was promise Abdul that I would keep trying because all I wanted was to have him home safe with us.

I managed to leave with an optimistic farewell, but as soon as I was in the car the tears and the aching chest came again. I put my head on the steering wheel and cried and cried until I noticed that some people inside the fence had put their heads out of their windows to check on me. That made me feel ashamed. How dare I, who was leaving that blighted place, be upset?

On returning to my home in Canberra that night, I settled and slept well for the first time in many months because I knew a very special person was already asleep in the house.

Chapter 18

A SPECIAL VISITOR

Ahad is Abdul's brother. Soon after making contact with him, I discovered he was only eighteen years old and in Year Ten at school in Brisbane. He was living in a group house with several other Hazara youths. I had a sense he was struggling, but it was hard to form any judgements from our few, brief telephone conversations. Ahad had arrived on Christmas Island by boat in 2011 when he was just fifteen. Since it would be easier for us to help Abdul together if we met each other face-to-face, I suggested we fly him down from Brisbane to visit us. I was blown away by his response.

'I would love to spend time in a family again.'

Those words revealed to me what this boy had been missing all these years. Although I had sent him some photos of my family, we were still complete strangers to him. For Ahad, this visit was an intrepid step, although not as intrepid as his journey to Australia.

We had arranged for Ahad to fly into Canberra the afternoon I returned from seeing Abdul, but as my plane arrived close to midnight I would have to wait until the morning to meet him.

'So, what's he like?' I asked Rob when he picked me up from the airport.

'He's a good-looking boy. Very strong-looking.' Rob put on his indicator and changed lanes. 'He doesn't say much, though. He's pretty shy.'

Rob described how he and Toby searched for Ahad for about half an hour after the plane arrived only to find him in the departure lounge.

'He had something to eat, but wanted to go to bed early. I guess he was tired.'

The following morning, I was waiting for Ahad in the kitchen when he crept in. I could immediately see what Rob meant when he said 'strong-looking'. Ahad had hard, built-up muscles, a severe crew cut and wore a leather biker jacket zipped right up to the throat. On the outside, he appeared formidable, even intimidating, but he was shy in this strange place, and I knew that first hello in the kitchen had taken a lot of effort. I could also see the sadness in his eyes.

Ahad later showed us photos of himself when he arrived as an unaccompanied child. He was a small, skinny boy with a lost look. In Afghanistan, a person's age is not recorded as precisely as it is in Western countries because it isn't as important a part of life as it is here. In fact, most Afghans don't know their actual birth date. Immigration usually assigns 31 December as the birthday for newly arrived asylum seekers, which is what they did for Ahad.

That morning, he told me that when he was first interviewed by immigration the officer cried because he looked so young and vulnerable. After spending five months in the Darwin detention centre, Ahad was finally recognised as a refugee and given permanent residency. He was moved to Brisbane, and allocated to a group house. It broke my heart to think that he had already spent three years in Australia like this.

Those two weeks of spring holidays in 2014 were spent with Ahad doing everyday family-holiday things in Canberra. We walked up Mount Ainslie, and when we got off the track and on to what my boys mournfully call 'Mum's long short-cuts', Ahad found his groove. Deftly bouncing over rocks and stones on the steep way down, he melted into the distance while I stumbled on, holding on to tree trunks for dear life.

We went to Floriade, the Canberra flower festival, and sat on the grass together in the sun. As we walked around the flowerbeds, I noticed his vigilance in scanning the crowds and wondered if it might offer a clue to what he had gone through.

One day on a bushwalk we were surprised by a huge brown snake lying on the grass so close to the path that Ahad nearly trod on it. He was shocked when I grabbed him, and then even more surprised to see the snake. It didn't take long for curiosity to override fear—and then I had to hold him back from investigating further. When Rob took Jasper and

Ahad on an 80-kilometre bike ride over the mountains to the coast, Ahad took this in his stride too.

But there were difficulties. Ahad's English was sometimes hard to understand and conversations were an effort on everyone's part. And while our boys were always friendly, and everyone tried their best to get along, we were all a little shy. Sometimes Ahad could look forbidding when his thoughts took him elsewhere, but when he smiled his eyes were always kind and receptive and I could see the cheeky and fun-loving boy inside. He proved to be a warm, generous, loyal and protective young man.

In the last few days before Ahad was to return to Brisbane, Rob and I were sitting together in the garden, watching the four boys throwing boomerangs and laughing at the dogs' puzzlement when the 'sticks' sometimes did a U-turn. Ahad's attachment to us had grown, and we had both seen him respond to the mothering I had offered to him. Rob and I had already discussed the possibility and I broached the subject again.

'So what about having the two of them here?' I said.

Without missing a beat, my generous and forbearing husband agreed again.

'Two,' he laughed. 'But no more!'

Just like that. It was simple.

I took Ahad for a long walk through the bush, trying to build up to asking if he wanted to stay with us. Eventually we sat on the ground in a clearing overlooking a creek. Overhead were tall ribbon gums and the ground was dotted with small daisies. We spoke for hours. I was worried that Ahad might feel put upon with this request and I didn't want him to feel uncomfortable—so the daisies around me were massacred as I tried to find the right words. When I did finally ask, he agreed straight away. I am sure it was a braver decision for him than it was for me.

We made plans then that Ahad would move in with us at the beginning of 2015 so he could first finish Year Eleven in Brisbane and go on a long-planned holiday. As part of the preparations for a change of school, I contacted his English teacher in Brisbane, who soon told me that in her opinion Ahad wouldn't amount to much. She complained that he didn't attend school wearing the correct school uniform or the correct leather school shoes, and the school didn't approve of his haircut. As if I cared about haircuts.

For years, the school had not realised that Ahad was an unaccompanied child living in a group house. I was shocked. How could this happen? How could a school make a judgement about learning abilities when it didn't know the child? Surely the fact that he was a refugee must have been a clue? The Ahad who stayed with us was intelligent and capable of much if given a chance. I thought homesickness and trauma were more important things to deal with than worrying about school shoes.

They also should have recognised that Ahad was chronically tired. Although he was only a schoolkid, he felt that he had to pay his own way in Australia. And because he wanted to be able to support his family back in Afghanistan, Ahad had worked every spare hour he had since arriving in Brisbane. In the holidays, he worked as a farm labourer picking onions, starting at 5 a.m. He also worked in an abattoir and a pizza shop during the school term.

As I got to know him better, more stories of neglect began to surface. He had some sort of youth worker—that is, someone was being paid to 'case manage' him—but this person didn't come to school for parent–teacher meetings, or any career guidance meetings. I can only assume that they had never communicated with the school about Ahad's circumstances. Worse still, there was an instance a few years before when Ahad had been mugged, beaten and left unconscious outside an ATM in Woodridge. He was told that his youth worker would come to check up on him in a few days but he told me no one ever did.

I regretted not meeting Ahad earlier. What he really needed was a family so he wouldn't have had to deal with everything on his own. There would have been time for more happiness, learning and fun. There would have been more time for him to do normal teenage things. The agencies that were supposed to look after Ahad had let him down.

After Ahad returned to Brisbane, we spoke on the phone and messaged each other. I wrapped and posted packets of homemade biscuits, and always popped a letter inside too.

Chapter 19

DATA BREACH

Back in February 2014, the immigration department had mistakenly published the personal details of 9258 asylum seekers. These details were online for eight and a half days, during which time the data was downloaded over 100 times by 100 different IP addresses. Abdul was one of those whose information was made public.

While the official statement by the department down-played the extent of the breach, it is not improbable that the Afghan government, the Taliban, Daesh and other criminal organisations would be interested in this type of information. The breach not only increased the risk to Abdul if he were sent back to Afghanistan by the Australian government, but it also increased the risk to his family.

Abdul was required to sign a document prepared by the department. It stated that 'some of your personal information may have been accessed' as a result of the report unintentionally uploaded by immigration to its website. The information included 'your name, date of birth, nationality, gender, details about your detention (when you were detained, reason and where) and if you have any other family members in detention'. He was told that 'the department will assess any implications for you personally as part of its normal processes'. There is no indication that Abdul had an interpreter or legal advice, or that any of these implications were discussed with him at any length, at the time of signing. Was this sixteen year old asked to sign this document to absolve the department of any responsibility should any repercussions arise from its mistake? Was this signature to make sure there were no impediments should the Australian government want to send him back to Afghanistan? Leaked data does not just disappear. Whoever took this data still has Abdul's details.

In late 2014, the then immigration minister, Scott Morrison, was having a sustained skirmish with the Senate in passing his Migration and Maritime Powers Legislation Amendment (Resolving the Asylum Legacy Caseload) Bill. He was selling this bill as a quick and cheap fix of the problem that had been allowed to brew: too many people, about 30,000, were languishing in detention and in the community without having their claims assessed. The main reason people were in this situation was that successive governments had chosen to stop processing asylum claims.

The bill was contentious, calling for the return of the Temporary Protection Visas (TPVs) briefly introduced by the Howard government in 1999, which gave refugees only three years' protection before they had to be reassessed. TPVs allowed no escape from the fear of being sent back to their home countries and they allowed no family reunion. They had likely increased the number of women and children, with no other way of reunion, boarding boats and increasing their risk of drowning at sea. TPVs also kept refugees in an indefinite limbo, with no stability or chance to move on with their lives. The bill also proposed to replace the Refugee Review Tribunal with a 'Fast-Track' refugee status determination. This would remove the checks and balances for the government in determining a person's refugee status and it undermined Australia's obligations to the Refugee Convention and the United Nations Convention on the Rights of the Child.

The minister offered a 'sweetener' to the Senate. If they passed the bill, he would release all children being held in mainland detention centres and on Christmas Island. Despite the incontrovertible evidence that holding children in prolonged detention was causing harm, he insisted that unless the bill was passed the children would stay put. Morrison, who could have released all children from detention centres with the stroke of his pen, was offering up these children, and their freedom, as a bargaining chip in his political game.

'Cruel, inhuman and unlawful punishment' is how the UN Committee Against Torture has described the offshore detention facility of Nauru, and yet the Minister's sweetener was not going to extend to the children trapped there. Despite their distress, known to the government through the harrow-ing documents of the Australian Human Rights Commission National Inquiry into Children in Immigration Detention 2014, and in the Moss Review, these kids on Nauru were to stay put no matter what the political outcome.

Because of this grubby trade-off, the bill kept being delayed in the Senate. The anguish of some politicians was painfully clear in the words of crossbench senator Ricky Muir: 'I am forced into a corner to decide between a bad decision or a worse decision.'

Abdul's diary at the time reflects some of his own torment:

Putting us in the cage does not mean we are safe. Actually I want to know what I did? If you try to be safe you will be a criminal? If you desire to fly you will become a criminal?

As a kid I used to tell them that I want to be pilot because I loved to fly and I thought flying mean going to air up from the earth. But now I understood that real flying is not that . . . real flying is the mind and thoughts flying . . . and when I come here I hoped that now its the time to fly. But they cut my wings and feathers and they put me in the cage.

Surely there is something seriously wrong with a govern-ment and its minister who are willing to trade the freedom of a child for the passing of a bill that itself would cause further harm? Surely the trading of human freedom is illegal? And surely, as a country, there must be something terribly wrong with us if we allow policies that we know are seriously damaging children to continue.

And yet . . .

Like the crossbench senators, I was torn. As a mum, and as a psychiatrist knowing full-well the harm of keeping children in detention, I wanted them out, but if this bill was passed into legislation it would harm so many others, including the very children who they purported to be saving.

All of my efforts to help Abdul had so far amounted to nothing. But if this one bill was passed, Abdul would probably be released. It was a bad deal—a really dirty deal—but it was the only hope we had. I waited and listened to the deliberations on the radio, and I read the paper every day, all the while hoping that it would be passed and worrying that it would.

Then, on 5 December 2014, the bill was finally passed and it was announced that most children would be released. There was relief, but there was no happiness, for freedom had come at a great cost to others. The next question was: would they allow Abdul to live with us?

Chapter 20

WINGS

After the bill was passed, we waited. Then I heard from the public servant I had been communicating with that we were being considered as an option for Abdul's community detention. With that exhilarating possibility came all the hoops we gladly jumped through: police checks, house checks, interviews with us and the children. Weeks passed and we still did not know if Abdul would be allowed to live with us; there was some mention from immigration of relocating him to Sydney. To distract myself, my solution was to scrub and declutter the house to within an inch of its life, even if it did drive Rob batty. I also wanted to make sure we passed scrutiny as suitable carers for Abdul, which was rather ironic, I thought, as I watched footage of the mouldy tents and dilapidated conditions of Nauru.

I remember one public servant trying to reassure me. 'If he doesn't live with you, you can visit him and take him out for dinner if you want to.' I know it was kindly meant, and I know that she was trying to make me feel better, but by this stage 'visiting' Abdul or 'taking him out for dinner' were just not enough. There was nothing I could do except hold on.

Running sustained me. On a Wednesday evening close to sunset, I took myself on a run up Mount Taylor. In Canberra, the bush capital, we are never more than ten minutes' walk away from the bush and the connecting, enlivening feel of dirt underfoot.

From the summit, I could see down to the Woden and Tuggeranong Valley town centres, while further in the distance the grey-green Brindabella Ranges, which cradle the city, were touched with apricot and gold from the setting sun. Further away I could see the individual peaks of Mount Ginini, Mount Gingera, Tidbinbilla and Camel's Hump, while closer by a mob of kangaroos stood around watching me. A cool breeze blew against my face and eagles circled in the evening sky.

I stood there for some time, feeling the warmth of the sun gradually fade as it disappeared over the horizon. Then, as I jogged slowly down the steep track, a brown wedge-tailed eagle swooped across my path just a few metres in front of me. She was so close I could see every overlapping feather of her wide, outstretched wings, and her stern dark eyes looked directly into mine. I felt that this magnificent being had flown down to make a connection, and inexplicably I knew I had been given a message of reassurance and contentment.

My conversations with Abdul began to turn to the practical and the real. He was anxious and several times asked me, 'What can I do to make myself better?'

I didn't really understand what he meant, so I asked him to explain.

'How can I improve my flaws?'

'Oh, Abdul. Don't worry, bub. You're good being just as you are. Being you. Of course it's going to be hard moving in with us and we're going to have to make it up as we go along.'

There was silence on his end of the telephone line.

'And we'll all need to give each other a lot of second chances.'

I could hear his quiet breathing before Abdul said, 'I will need guidance.'

To which I replied, 'Me too.'

xxxxxxx

I will be forever thankful to the anonymous angels in the Department of Immigration who listened to our pleas and allowed Abdul to stay with us. As it felt to us, he was finally coming home. Abdul would take the Virgin Airways flight 1354 from Darwin to Sydney and then the VA672 Sydney to Canberra flight, arriving on the evening of 22 December 2014.

Chapter 21

A LETTER TO ZAYNAB

The most important person I had to seek permission from before the boys moved in was their mother, Zaynab. The following letter is one I gave to Ahad to translate and read to his mum in his regular phone calls to her. Ahad had already visited us for two weeks in spring and at the time I wrote this Abdul was still languishing in detention.

Dear Zaynab,

It is so hard to find the right words. I hope that in translation this says what I want to say to you. For now, the only common language we have is being mothers. So I hope Ahad translates every word for you . . . even if he thinks it might be embarrassing, or maybe not 100% correct!! Okay, Ahad?

I want you to know how much I respect you and care about you and your family. And I want to reassure you that I will do what I can to give your boys all the family and mothering/aunty support they need when they are in Australia until you and everyone else can get here. I hope I can be a useful support in your absence. It will be a pleasure for us, not a burden, as you have lovely, lovely boys.

They are so attached to you, and I know from both of them they love you so much that I hope you never ever worry that I am undermining your relationship with them. My respect for you and what you have done for your children is part of what has motivated me; it is your work that has meant they have turned out so wonderfully!

I am so so sorry and ashamed that my country has not been kind to your boys. They have so much potential, and are such beautiful and special people, that we must be a nation of idiots not to open our arms to them. And I am sorry that this is the worst Australia has ever been to refugees at any point in time.

It was fate that connected Abdul and me in Darwin last year. I was not meant to be there (I was filling the role for someone else) and I think he may have come to the visitors' room by chance too. My focus that day was talking to the pregnant women and women with babies. I am a psychiatrist and my specialty is helping mums and babies. I am so glad that I got to meet Abdul. My first impression of him was that he has grown up surrounded with love and support (that was you!), and that his brain needs all the education/exercise it can get!

Over time, and after getting to know Abdul, there is no doubt of my initial impression, but now I am attached as well.

I hope you do not mind that I think of him as one of my kids—
this is why I am trying so hard to get him out of detention. Abdul
is struggling at the moment, I am sad to say. Being locked
up does that to people. But he isn't broken. He has a very
strong spirit and is incredibly patient, and a lot kinder about
the people who make his life hard than I could ever be. He is
very gracious and very clever. With only a little support and
freedom, Abdul could achieve anything he put his mind to.

Maybe I won't say as much about Ahad because he
may feel uncomfortable reading this to you? But I am also
thanking fate that I met him. I didn't know too much about
Ahad before he came to visit and didn't know who to expect.
We are getting to know each other. He is a lovely steady
young man. I think Ahad is closer to my boys in nature. He is
socially cautious, but this may be because he has had to be
more self-reliant than any teenager ought to be in the last few
years. He has had to face many difficulties alone, but he has
done well. What I see of Ahad is a courageous, intelligent and
capable young man. I am really looking forward to him being
a part of our family next year. As well as helping him study
year 12, I think we all will have a lot of fun!

So now a little about us. My husband Robert (Rob) and I
have three boys. Jasper is 15, Lucas is 12 and Toby is now
11. Rob is a man who gets things done without a fuss. He is
my rock. He was very adventurous (before we had children)
and has explored through Canada, America and Australia by
bike. We met nineteen years ago when we were both doctors
working in the emergency department. I was taken by how
polite and kind he was to patients and how much respect he

had in the hospital. He has been the best father to our boys. He is supportive of me. His parents were refugees from Hungary and arrived here in 1967. Rob was born two months later at an immigration centre in Sydney. He did not speak English until he started school, and had to learn pretty quickly! This may help to understand why we have offered this opportunity to your boys.

Jasper is also a quiet young man. He is intelligent and is very interested in science and engineering. He has been spending a lot of time in our shed making things . . . some of which have given me grey hair! Unfortunately, last weekend he gave himself some very nasty burns on his hand. But from another point of view, he is very very lucky to not have more damage. In some ways, I think this was a very useful wake-up call that parental advice is not always boring and stupid.

Lucas is very quick-witted. He uses language very skilfully, but sometimes it gets him into trouble! He is kind-hearted and generous. When he puts his mind to it, and is committed, he can accomplish amazing things.

Toby has incredible persistence and strength. He is also very smart and organised. He is very loyal and kind to his friends and this is lovely to see.

We all try to have fun together as a family. We like the outdoors and music, but we are also very focused on our boys doing as well as they can academically as well as being kind people. Life should not be a competition and being of good character is the most important thing.

It is hard to describe our children in just a few words, isn't it? I hope this gives you an idea of what sort of family we are, along with Ahad's report.

A letter to Zaynab

I have been trying to read and learn as much about Afghanistan's history and present as I can. What I am realising is that as much as I am learning, the more I need to learn!

What we would like to do is welcome your boys into our family to become one of us. Until you arrive, we will give them all the family support and love they want. With us, they will have an intensive course in English and Australian culture, as well as our focus on education and learning.

It is my belief that strong culture keeps people strong, too. We don't know too much about your culture and language, but want our house to be culturally safe, meaning that your boys still keep pride in their culture and language, and we support and celebrate that.

One day, I would like to Skype with you, to be able to see you and the family and talk the best we can.

I hope that soon all my efforts in trying to get Abdul out of detention will work. Then, when your boys are staying here, you will not need to worry. We can look forward together to the next thing, which is meeting each other in person! One day we will just sit here together in Canberra—I can see us sitting under a tree while Abdul makes some tea. We will learn some of each other's languages and be happy.

Love, Emma
(and Rob, Jasper, Lucas and Toby)

Chapter 22

WAITING AT THE AIRPORT

Everyone was excited to see Abdul, but as a family of six we couldn't all fit into the car, so it was left to Toby and me to collect him. We arrived at Canberra airport way too early because Toby, the most adventurous of us, was so excited to see his new brother—which is how he chose to see Abdul from the beginning.

I have often wondered what Abdul was thinking on that long flight. A more fortunate person may see travel across the world as an adventure or a holiday. Abdul's journey certainly wasn't. I imagine leaving home in Afghanistan must have been the hardest thing he had ever done and each leg of his journey presented another danger with more risks and more troubles. Until he reached Australia, nowhere would be truly safe. But the rules had also changed during his travels and

Abdul's arrival on Christmas Island hadn't secured him the longed-for safety but indefinite imprisonment instead. That was, until now. But in truth, moving in with us in a strange city in a foreign country was another unknown for Abdul.

Toby, chatty with expectation, and I sat in the almost empty arrivals hall and watched the comings and goings of groups of tired-looking travellers, most of whom appeared to be public servants walking purposefully out to waiting cars. Before long we turned the scrutiny of each new arrival into a game to pass the time. Perhaps Abdul was that big bald man with the loud shirt? Or that hipster guy with the big moustache and guitar case? That cranky-looking woman dragging a large shopping bag through the door probably wasn't Abdul . . . until, eventually, the flow of people stopped and the doors remained closed. I started to worry. Maybe someone at immigration had changed his or her mind again about letting Abdul stay with us? That idea was not improbable, and my anxiety rose until finally he walked through the doors.

Strangely, I hardly recognised Abdul, which made me start doubting myself. After all, I told myself, I have only visited him on three occasions. Maybe this boy is not Abdul? This boy seems smaller than I remember and he's holding himself stiffly. This boy isn't smiling the same warm way Abdul does, but he is holding his right elbow with his left hand, which means his shoulder must also have been dislocated too . . . This boy is carrying a large zippered storage bag and is now clutching a backpack to his chest. It's making it hard for me to hug him . . .

Maybe he was wearing long pants and a red T-shirt. One thing I do remember clearly is that all I wanted to do was to take him with us and speed off home, away from the airport and away from the guard accompanying him. Inside my head I was screaming at this person, 'Go away already. Your job is finished. No more rules or bureaucracy. *Let's. Just. Go! Now!'* I also had to restrain myself—which I knew was weird but related to an outpouring of maternal instinct—from an urge to count all of Abdul's fingers and toes.

And there was also another feeling: a physical sense of joy. Abdul was here, now, in Canberra, and he was to live with us! He had finally come home.

xxxxxxx

When we got back to the house, I must have showed Abdul his room and hands must have been shaken all around. I know we involved the boys in showing him the bathroom, and we introduced the dogs, but apart from that I don't remember much of his first night. I think I was too overwhelmed.

I try to imagine what Abdul's first night in the 'real' Australia was like for him—not the barbed-wire world of the detention centres. What was his first dinner in Australia like? It must have been different from the institutional food of the previous 500 days and different from the food he existed on during his journey across the seas. It most certainly would not have been what his mother had cooked for him in Afghanistan.

I can picture Abdul on that first night sitting between Toby and me at our kitchen table. The rest of us are speaking happy, noisy and 'arguey' family dinner-table English, not the English of the guards or the immigration department officials in the detention centre. Not even the English of his teachers at school. Abdul looks a little lost. Only later would he tell me that he had no idea what we were talking about.

None of the four boys sitting at our table that night knew what they were in for, but they all tried hard from the beginning. In fact, I think it was my boys who did the most work in welcoming Abdul properly at the beginning. I was too busy worrying about getting things right.

Chapter 23

FREEDOM ISN'T JUST WALKING OUT THE DOOR

Ahad was not due to move in until the end of the summer holidays, and in those first few weeks with us Abdul was quiet and cautious, as if he was looking for the catch in this deal. His responses were always polite, always saying 'whatever you want' when anyone asked him for his preference. He played games with Toby, but was reserved with the older boys. He barely said anything to Rob.

Although he would accompany us for all the touristy excursions I organised for him, and the four boys would dutifully accompany me to the shops, Abdul otherwise stuck to the house like a limpet. A few times his exuberant spirit shone through, like when we all went out to a concert of two cellos playing rock music and he was out of his seat and head-banging AC/DC with the best of them! Perhaps he just could not yet fathom his freedom. I didn't know if growing up in Afghanistan had failed to foster the practice of walking in public for fun, but I did know that being stuck behind a wire fence for seventeen months wouldn't have given Abdul a good sense of what was on the other side.

xxxxxxx

In detention, Abdul had heard a lot about the threatening, hateful discourse against Muslims and asylum seekers on television, radio and Facebook and other social media in Australia, and later told me that this had been playing on his mind when he first moved in with us. The violent consequences of hate and racism in Afghanistan were what he had fled from, and with Ahad having already been beaten up in Brisbane, Abdul still didn't know what to expect on the streets of Canberra.

A rather horrible psychological research program in the United States in the 1960s that would be unconscionable now involved caged dogs being given random electric shocks. The dogs, who were trapped inside the cages, gave up trying to escape because they had learned that nothing they could do would stop the shocks. Later, even when the doors were left open and the dogs could leave their cages, they didn't. This behaviour was termed 'learned helplessness', and I wondered if some of Abdul's reluctance to explore on his own, and not use his newfound freedom, was a similar response.

This boy, who had only just turned seventeen, had been through a lot: the emotional and cultural shock of leaving

Afghanistan, his journey through Dubai, Sri Lanka and Indonesia, and 500 days in immigration detention had all progressively eroded his mental reserves.

I returned to work after the Christmas break and wasn't able to take Abdul out as much as before. After I realised that Abdul had been sitting in the house for several days, Rob and I were both concerned about his getting cabin fever. We told him he needed to go out for a walk. In retrospect, maybe we pushed too hard that day because Abdul obviously wasn't keen and was dragging his feet. By the time he set off, it was already late afternoon.

Half an hour after he left, a loud, violent hammering began on the roof. Outside our cosy kitchen's window the ground disappeared under a blanket of white marbles. Rob and I looked at each other contritely. A hailstorm challenge was not what we had planned for Abdul's first solo outing, but we were confident he could look after himself because he had been through worse physical challenges. When he finally arrived home some hours later, dripping wet, he told us that he'd had to hide under a bridge and had then become lost.

This ordeal—maybe it was an initiation—seemed to be a turning point for Abdul. Despite his shivering, he was chipper and chatty. He had pushed through the barrier of leaving our house.

That night Abdul stayed up with Rob and me to watch television. After a short while, he fell asleep, and for the first time we saw his face at peace. He looked so very young. This brought back the cosy memories of early parenthood, and

Rob and I gazed warmly at each other as I gently ruffled the hair of this sleeping boy.

I had demanded a lot of commitment from Rob in this venture and had worried that he might not feel he could do it. But with the look he gave me I knew he was in this with me. We had done the right thing.

Abdul slept on after the movie ended. The problem was what to do now? Did we disturb him so he could go to bed or did we leave him and risk him waking up in this new place scared and disoriented? We chose to sit beside him in the dark and watch him sleep, while my heart swelled with love for the beautiful, kind, gentle and generous man, my husband.

xxxxxxx

It was not until a few weeks later that I saw a diary entry that Abdul had left on my computer when he was sitting at our kitchen table. I caught my breath for it was then that I truly realised how hard Abdul was trying.

lesson of life—december 2014

once upon a time there was a boy with lots of ambitions he wanted to do what he want but he didn't want to make any mistake.

he didn't know that its right to do mistake as far as he can learn something from his mistake and not repeating the same thing again. because he was scared of the people who could make fun of him and he didn't know that he need to break those barrier just by ignoring them and that was his mistake.

119

he was a good boy but mostly he was doing what other people like it even he didn't like it.

because he was enjoying to see others happy and they are living in peace. and what ever he was doing he didn't want anybody know how he is feeling about everything especially when he was trying to help some body because he was thinking differently and usually he didn't know how to express his feeling.

But he knew that whatever he is doing its right

We thought we were being friendly and kind, but he was still uneasy with us. Abdul might have been out from behind the wire fence, but for him each step in this new place had so much riding on it.

Chapter 24

OUR ANCESTORS' WOUNDS

I understand that many Australians against refugees, or asylum seekers, or even more specifically asylum seekers arriving by boat, are often afraid that foreigners, especially from Muslim countries, will change their culture and 'way of life'. But what is Australian culture anyway and why should the luck of just being born here give a person the right to decide what this culture should be? Applying that logic, I suppose I should be calling the shots because my family roots are deeply connected to the land. Many of my ancestors were the earliest boat people to arrive in Australia, while others arrived here 60,000 years ago.

My great-great-great-great-great grandmother was a boat person. Elizabeth Goldsmith was a convict who arrived on the female convict ship the *Lady Juliana*, between the first and the second fleets, and was one of the first European women to set foot on Australian soil. Other ancestors, some who escaped the Irish famine, also arrived by boat from England many generations ago—today they might be dismissed as 'economic migrants' because they were starving and destitute and wanted to make a better life for themselves.

My great-grandmother on my father's side was also called Emma. We don't know why, but as a baby she was removed from her family in Grenfell in western NSW. In my walks through the bush with my grandmother, she told me that Emma, her mother, lived with a white 'foster' mother. This woman beat Emma and made her work as a servant for the family. My grandmother was proud of her Aboriginal ancestry, but she was also scared of revealing it to her children. In those days, children deemed 'half-caste' were still being taken from their families.

Some years ago, when my dad told me his computer password was 'Wiradjuri' (sorry, Dad, now you're going to have to change it), I felt a pang of grief that he still associates this part of himself with privacy and secrets. This may seem banal and irrelevant, but it has meant that the connection to identity and culture has been stifled. We still don't know if we even are Wiradjuri, but we are certainly Koori.

For some people in my family, our Aboriginal heritage remains discomforting. They claim that our dark eyes and olive skin came from an unknown Spaniard, or that Emma was the baby of a South Sea princess who fell off a ship! Anything to deny Aboriginality. On my mother's side, too, there were whispers that we had 'a touch of the tar brush'—such an appalling term. My dark-skinned maternal great-grandfather was raised by his mother, 'Pidge', who was a shearer's cook. There was no paper record of who she was when I tried to find her.

Racism has shaped my family's history: in the genocide of Aboriginal people, being driven off their land, and in the Stolen Generations. Hidden in the landscape itself is the knowledge of what really happened to many of my ancestors. Racism has also caused loss of knowledge, language and culture, and, as such, has carved deep wounds. For my father, there was no path in his youth to reconnect with his stolen culture and language.

I am certainly not pretending I have had the hardships that many generations are still suffering right now, because I am one of the lucky ones. I have not had the immediate pain of being removed from my family—as happened to my great-grandmother—nor have my children been taken from me. And because I have fair skin I have been shielded from the vilest racist attacks, but I know full well what people say and how they behave. These things add up and cause a sickness in the soul. Unlike many, I have also had the privilege of education and of healing, but make no mistake: because of my ancestors' wounds, my spirit, like many other Aboriginal people, has been marked with scars.

Research in the last decade has shown us that memories of trauma and fear may be passed down not just through memories and stories but through direct gene modification in a process called epigenetics. A parent's or even a grandparent's trauma can affect the brain function of the next generations.

Generations of trauma and loss, and generations of parents with no experience of being parented themselves, have affected the psyche of many Aboriginal communities and families, including my own. The personal 'not knowing' and never experiencing what one has lost does not protect one from grief. In fact, it makes the pain confusing and harder to reconcile. Any woman who has lost a baby she never had a chance to hold can confirm this truth.

The Bengali poet Rabindranath Tagore wrote, 'When I stand before thee at the day's end thou shalt see my scars and know that I had my wounds and also my healing.' Scars remind us of things that should never be forgotten, but they also show us that we can heal. The scars I inherited have given me strength and purpose, and they make me notice things and take action. But sometimes even that is not enough.

xxxxxxx

Back in December 2013, the day before I was due to visit the detention centres on my first visit to Darwin, I found myself waiting outside the hospital for a few hours while my colleagues had meetings. After the long flight cooped up in the plane, I was very happy to sit outside and read a book. After a while, some young Aboriginal women from the Tiwi Islands sat beside me on the bench. We yarned and pretty soon— as is often the way—we realised we knew some people in common. As we were talking, they lit up their cigarettes, and within a few moments a Serco guard loomed over us, rudely telling the girls to put their smokes out. Pulling on both my mum and doctor hat, and trying to smooth over the unpleasantness of this man's manner, I brought up the health risks of smoking. When the girls found out I was a doctor they seemed to be more interested in and surprised about that than anything I had to say about the dangers of smoking.

As we sat sipping our bottles of iced tea and yarning in the sunshine, I encouraged them to think big and follow their dreams of education—one of the girls wanted to be a nurse—until the Serco guard interrupted us again. This time he accused the young women of concealing alcohol in their bottles of iced tea before harshly ordering them to 'shove off'.

Interesting that this man didn't order me to leave, or accuse me of hiding alcohol in my bottle. But, of course, I didn't 'look' Aboriginal. At the time, I made the assumption that hospital security was acquainted with the young women so I didn't interfere. Later, I discovered that Serco didn't supply hospital security and that this fellow must have only been at the hospital to guard an asylum seeker receiving medical treatment. He was just flexing his authoritarian muscles. When I finally understood the situation the following day, I was ashamed that I hadn't spoken up.

There is, of course, a proud history, albeit largely unknown, of Aboriginal people standing up to protect others. In the 1800s, after Europeans crossed the Great Dividing Range into the park-like land around the Bathurst region in central western NSW, my ancestor's hunting and farming grounds were destroyed and people starved, while many lives were lost through brutal attacks, deliberate poisonings and massacres. When Aboriginal people fought back, martial law was declared. As the war continued, the Wiradjuri warrior

Windradyne saw the destruction of his people and knew he had to end the hostilities. Wearing a straw hat with the word 'Peace' written on it, Windradyne walked over 200 kilometres through the bush, across the Blue Mountains, to Sydney, where in 1824 he offered to sit down with the enemy, Governor Brisbane, to negotiate. His bravery and diplomacy likely saved many of his people and his legacy is one all Australians can share and call our own.

The Australia that I have in my heart is the land and society where people have had to be resourceful, hardworking and creative. We are a laid-back people, relaxed, and generally accepting of differences. We have also been kind and generous to those in need and brave in defending them—but there is a darker side to our history and psyche.

Since the first lie of *terra nullius*—the declaration that there were no people here when the English arrived—many Australians have tried to ignore the existence of an entire race, and there have been those, including our governments and politicians, who have ignored the massacres and looked for ways to hide, or legitimise, unconscionable acts. While thinking about this history of 'turning away from an ugly truth', I have begun to wonder if it might be one of the reasons such disgraceful choices regarding asylum seekers and refugees, both onshore and offshore, have gone largely unchallenged by so many of my fellow Australians today.

I am who I am, and deep in my soul is knowledge of loss and what can happen if we ignore another's essential humanity. Perhaps the sense of recognition and connection I shared with Abdul is associated with this? Perhaps it is deep within our DNA: like a double helix, where our ancestors' stories of sadness and loss are entwined. His story, like my ancestors' stories, reflects the way racism destroys lives. He, too, has his scars.

Who I am is precious, and while I do not have any authority to speak on behalf of Aboriginal people, I do have a responsibility to speak out against racism and injustice wherever I see it. I am also, very simply, an Australian woman, and as an Australian woman I can't—and won't—remain silent when children suffer.

Chapter 25

THE CORN TRAIL

Until a day in January 2015, which we all now describe as 'The Corn Trail Day', I don't think my positive thoughts about our decision to welcome Abdul into our family had really been tested.

The Corn Trail winds down the Great Dividing Range through Monga National Park and down to the Bolaro Valley near the south coast of NSW. It was named for the supplies of corn that packhorses brought along the trail. It was also a route for livestock and for the gold prospectors in the NSW gold rush in the nineteenth century. But the route is more ancient than this. For many thousands of years, it was the path Aboriginal people travelled between the coast and tablelands.

Toby, Abdul and I started our walk on an uncharacteristically cool and misty January day: beautiful weather for an amble. We sauntered through forests of massive eucalyptus trees and paths fringed with leathery coral ferns. Along the way, we looked for the rare Monga waratah, a small shrub with dark-green, lance-shaped leaves and delicate, wiry red flowers bright enough to look like beacons in the distance. Some of the trail was flooded and the boys flitted across each pond, while I took longer, traversing the water by balancing on logs and stones. Before the steady downhill section, the trail zigzagged along ridges and the saddles between mountain peaks. The day became sunny and warm as the mist cleared.

Toby and Abdul were in front and I was enjoying their lighthearted banter. Toby was enamoured with this new older brother who spent so much time with him, and Abdul was playful and remarkably patient with Toby, who was usually fizzing with excitement.

A rocky outcrop beside the path provided a view across the mountains. This place—a platform of ancient splintered rocks—gave me a sense of recognition. Some places communicate like this. But it also grew a feeling in the base of my stomach and the back of my neck and throat that I should not be there, and just at that moment I narrowly missed stepping on a brown snake basking on the rocks. This venomous snake seemed like an omen, and the memory of the near miss lingered for the rest of the day. I was unsure if this was a kindly warning or something else.

The boys, oblivious to my brush with the snake, were keen to press on. They both moved swiftly down the rocky slopes, enjoying their athletic prowess. I walk-jogged behind, content that they were immersed in their world of freedom and play. After half an hour, I indicated that I was stopping behind a log to pee and I signalled for them to go ahead.

'Don't look back, don't turn back,' I called, worried that Abdul may not understand and come back for me. We were still getting to know each other, and as far as toilet business was concerned I did not want any miscommunication.

When I finished, I jogged for a while in an attempt to catch up. With no sign of them, I picked up my pace and ran steadily for fifteen minutes. Still no sign. Surely they weren't running that fast? Surely they would have waited? I was on a saddle between two peaks in dense forest. In the distance, all I could see was a solid blue-green of distant mountains and wilderness. My calls became louder and louder until I remembered our emergency whistle. Each time I blew it— the noise was loud enough to hurt my ears—I would strain to listen, but only bird call and creaking trees replied. By now I had not seen the boys for almost an hour.

'Okay, this is serious and panicking won't help. You need to be sensible,' I told myself. 'You haven't had food or drink for two hours, and you can't think properly if you're tired.'

Fighting the urge to keep running, I sat down and made myself drink and eat some squares of chocolate. When I finished, my plan was to jog on slowly for another 30 minutes.

So far, the path had been clearly marked, meaning there was little chance they would have taken a wrong turn. Surely they would turn back if they had? Every five minutes I blasted the whistle. In the silence that followed, I realised that sound does not travel well around mountains, and of course, with no reception, mobile phones are useless.

By this stage, the boys had been gone for nearly two hours and I remembered a horrible anguish from the past. When Toby was three years old, I had made a quick trip to the shops to buy icy poles. Rob and the boys had been playing in the house, but on my return Toby was nowhere to be found. For an hour, our neighbours and the family frantically searched our house and garden, raced around the streets and, most horribly, checked the stormwater drains, until Rob, himself still shaking from the ordeal, brought our son home in his arms. Rob had found him, wet-eyed and holding a dripping banana Paddle Pop, sitting on the lap of the checkout girl at our local shopping centre. Toby, my little boy, had only wanted to follow me to the shops. To this day, it still physically hurts to think of those busy roads he crossed and the 'what-ifs'.

Toby was still my baby boy and I screamed out for him in the bush. By then, my fears were focused on a range of disastrous scenarios: he'd been badly hurt, bitten by a snake, fallen down the side of the mountain, or had become lost and I would have no idea how to ever find him. How could I save my baby? At that point, I realised I hadn't been calling out Abdul's name. I wasn't as upset for him, nor had I been worried about his vulnerability. Rather illogically, I supposed that if he had got through all he had, nothing else could happen to him now . . .

My anxiety had led my brain through all sorts of other dreadful scenarios and some of them, I am ashamed to say, even included Abdul harming Toby. I recognised that these thoughts were irrational. Why on earth would this boy travel all this way to Australia and endure what he had just so he could push my child down the side of a mountain? Fear and a sense of not being in control is fertile ground for mistrust to grow.

To fight my growing panic, I stopped again for water, chocolate and rest. Watching ants carrying sticks back to their nest was a distraction until I could focus again. It would be dark in a few hours. I needed to go back to the car and get help, so after calling out their names a few more times I made the excruciating decision to turn around, leaving my boys on the trail

As it turned out, when I had stopped for a wee, Toby and Abdul had raced on ahead. When they reached the river, they had skipped stones across the clear, flowing water, then happily ate their lunch under the rainforest canopy as they waited for me. Toby had reassured Abdul when he asked about me: 'Mum doesn't get lost, she's okay.'

Eventually Abdul persuaded Toby that they should turn back and look for me. By this time, Toby was tired, but Abdul looked after him, cajoling and entertaining him all the way back.

The story ends this way. I heard footsteps behind me. When I turned, the first thing I saw was Abdul smiling at me with relief. He told me that he had been worried and that he'd heard my screams a few minutes before. When he saw me crying, though, he thought something had happened to me. Toby arrived a few metres behind him, looking nonplussed, his dark, unruly curls falling over his brow.

I gathered Toby into my arms and held him tight. But as I hugged him, my uneasiness did not immediately evaporate.

Blaydin detention centre, 40 kilometres outside Darwin, when I first visited with ChilOut in December 2013.

The back entrance of Blaydin, when I visited again in 2014. This was the most 'welcoming' of the two detention centres in the same location. The other centre, Wickham, was surrounded by two sets of high wire fences that could be electrified.

Abdul inside Blaydin, 2014. Cameras and phones were not allowed inside the compound and I was lucky to take this photograph while waiting for the guards to let me in.

Pallets of baby goods left outside Blaydin detention centre in the tropical heat and rain.

With Abdul and Ahad in Sydney, 2015.

With my youngest
son, Toby, as well,
Brisbane, 2015.

Abdul and Toby at the beginning of the Corn Trail walking track. Little did I know how this day would turn out.

Abdul and Tony on a day trip to the beach.

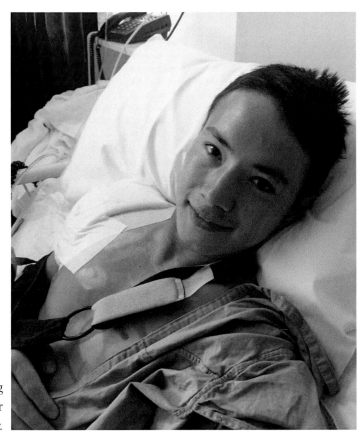

Abdul recovering from shoulder surgery.

Get well soon: the boys kept Abdul company in those first few days of recovery.

Swimming with Jasper,
despite the op!

Rob and I are
still smiling,
two decades on.

Driving lessons. This was Abdul's idea of helping me navigate through congested Melbourne traffic. It is never boring with this guy around!

On the road again, this time on bikes in the middle of Deua National Park.

Climbing Mt Kosciuszko. The boys felt on top of the world—they said it reminded them of where they came from in the mountains of Afghanistan.

Abdul, with Lucas and Toby on a sailing boat trip. Now, boat trips are fun; this boy has come a long way!

Perhaps I had offended some deep-down order of things? Was the snake a warning that opening our home and life to this other boy was a step into chaos? I questioned what Abdul was doing in our family. What if there had been an accident? Would I have been able to give Abdul as much forgiveness as my other boys? And what if something had happened to Abdul?

I knew he was a gentle person with a beautiful soul and that the thoughts I had on the trail were ridiculous. Perhaps this was all the sort of misplaced and unexamined anxiety that contributes to the paranoia and anger about refugees in our community. If it is, then I feel sorry for these people, because it is an uncomfortable and unnecessary feeling. Abdul later told me that all he remembers of the reunion was how I ignored him.

I still regret the pain my doubt caused him. If I could change anything about that day (apart from getting separated in the first place), it would have been to hold Abdul tight, the way I had held Toby, and I would have thanked him for being a caring big brother.

We know that there must be a bond of trust. We know we can't take these journeys without trusting our team. There will be lots of bad days and there will be more tests of our endurance. The point is to keep going.

Chapter 26

THE FACE OF THE IMMIGRATION DEPARTMENT

Abdul had been transferred into our care under the rules of community detention. The immigration department never regarded us as foster parents or even guardians; rather we were Community Link 'custodians' and had to enforce his ongoing detention in the community. This was a massive improvement from being locked up without any end in sight, but Abdul was still not free. There were exhaustive rules and constraints, not just for Abdul but for all of us as a family.

There was a 9 p.m. curfew, which in practice meant that movies were out, concerts were out, family dinners at friends' places were out, along with evening sports, like touch footy. These normal activities were closed to Abdul and, by association, to the rest of us. Abdul was not allowed to stay anywhere else but our house overnight, and Rob or myself always had to be at home with him each night. There went our family camping trips on the weekend.

If we did want a night away, or a holiday, we had to go through a complex bureaucratic process, which took ten working days to authorise. We could not apply directly to immigration but only through Abdul's youth worker. On more than one occasion, I had to frantically call around the night before to chase the missing approval for a pre-planned holiday or risk being accused of wrongdoing.

Our biggest worry was that if we broke the rules, even a little, then immigration would remove Abdul from our care. This especially concerned me because it seemed to me that they were looking for any excuse to lock him up again or send him back to Afghanistan. And, of course, in the background Nauru and Manus Island always loomed.

These restrictions may not seem like much compared with being locked up in detention, but they added to the psychological pressure on Abdul and served as a constant reminder of the power that the immigration department still had over him.

Shortly after he came to live with us, Abdul was summonsed to meet his immigration case manager. I insisted that I accompany him, determined he would not face this alone. As a psychiatrist, I have been helping people with disability support, housing, Veterans Affairs, workplace injuries and welfare payments long enough to know that vulnerable people are sometimes not treated well by people in the public service.

We arrived at the immigration office at the appointed time, but the door was locked. The security guard told us that the public were not allowed in for another twenty minutes. When we explained that we had an appointment, he told us that the case manager didn't see people until the office opened. Okay, I thought, it was odd for his case manager to order someone to come in at a time knowing they would have to wait, but we would remain unrelentingly patient and polite. We waited with the growing group of people gathering outside.

Eventually Abdul and I were allowed to enter. The young receptionist received us with a snarl, but, to be fair, it was how she treated everybody who came in that morning. She told us that our wait was going to be extended because the case manager was busy. There were a few other people waiting and I exchanged a smile with another man, who seemed as wryly amused as I was. As I looked around the room that day, I realised that the asylum seekers were all easily identifiable: they were the ones who seemed frozen, with still faces and closed-off eyes.

When the receptionist finally called Abdul's name, we entered an austere grey office that reminded me of a police interview room. The case manager spoke to Abdul in an accusatory tone. Surely, I thought, this person has read Abdul's file and knows his story? Did she not see how the traumatised boy shrank into his chair looking small and scared? I was shell-shocked, I suppose, and stayed quiet. Why, I kept wondering, was she being so mean? But when she joked that Abdul's time in Darwin was like a holiday camp, I'd had enough.

'I don't think Abdul had "fun" there. In fact, it's very unpleasant to be locked up not knowing when or if you'll leave,' I said. 'It's a fact that kids in detention have been psychologically damaged by this experience. The longer they're there, the worse it is, and Abdul was there for over 500 days.'

The case manager snapped back at me: 'If you make accusations like that in public we will charge you with slander.' Bubbles of her foamy spit landed on the paperwork. After wiping them away with her finger, she looked up and gave what I think was a smile to Abdul, adding, 'You can call me if you have any problems. I am here to help.'

As we walked back to the car, Abdul noticed the tears I was trying to hide and put his arm around me.

'That's why I didn't want you to come and have them talk to you like that,' he said. 'I'm used to it. It's how immigration is.'

Chapter 27

BOYS REUNITED

I can't imagine what it was like for Ahad and Abdul as children to have to say goodbye to each other believing it could be forever, but in February 2015 they were eventually reunited. The brothers had not seen each other for over four years. Ahad had spent the Christmas holidays working and taking a holiday with friends, and his moving in with us had been delayed several times. Perhaps he had some second thoughts about the move, but now he was ready to start the new school year with us.

Abdul and I drove to the airport to pick him up. Leaving the house with Abdul could be a frustrating exercise. He tended to see departure times as a reminder to have a shower before getting dressed and packed, before asking sweetly as I was foot-tapping at the door, bag over shoulder, if I would like a cup of tea. 'You look like you need some sugar in your blood,' he might tell me. This time, however, he was well and truly ready, and reminded me more than once about the time.

Drives in the car with Abdul were usually noisy and colourful. He had learned the game Spotto from the boys (you yell out 'Spotto!' on seeing a yellow car), but he added more volume and his own special variations for every colour of car, including the white ones, always poking me in the shoulder each time. There is usually singing, followed by mock exasperated requests from me to 'pipe down for crying out loud!' This time, though, Abdul only stared out the window, still and quiet, as we slipped through the suburbs, past Parliament House, the 'Bugs Bunny' statue outside the Defence headquarters and Lake Burley Griffin.

We arrived at the airport right on time, and there was Ahad, walking out the arrival doors, all as planned.

As I saw him, I realised I hadn't thought it all through as much as I should have. I should have parked instead of using the drop-off zone, because I was sitting in the driver's seat and could not get out and greet Ahad. It also meant that Abdul's first hug with his brother had the pressure of waiting cars building up behind him. They embraced, but not as extravagantly as I would have expected, and then after dealing with the bags and working out who should sit where in the car, we drove home. I smiled as I looked back in the rear-view mirror at the two brothers speaking quietly together in Hazaragi.

When we got home, I wanted Abdul and Ahad to have time together without feeling obliged to include all of us, so

I had set up an activity if they wanted to make a new garden bed outside. I thought this would make a space for them: side-by-side in the garden on a lovely late-summer afternoon. There was only one mattock and I could see the boys taking turns, revealing a long-established pattern of being together and sharing. From time to time, I came out to give them cups of tea and biccies, and then, after a few hours, I persuaded them to stop and come inside.

At dinner, Jasper, Lucas and Toby were playful, asking questions about the world and trying to get a conversation going, bickering among themselves and telling jokes. It was a happy show of 'us-ness' and their gestures were an inviting-in. Abdul also joined in and helped Ahad by explaining things for him. Ahad was pleasant and polite with us, but I could tell that it would take some time before he would feel like he belonged with us the way I hoped he would.

That evening, I tiptoed into their room to see if they would like some tea only to find the two boys curled up together, asleep like puppies. This moment touched my soul with joy, and if there was one thing I could have wished for it would have been for their mother to have seen this too.

Chapter 28

CONNECTING

I never expected to have five teenage boys. *Have* is not the right word. As the poet Khalil Gibran wrote, 'Your children are not your children . . . They come through you but not from you / And though they are with you yet they belong not to you.' So, although I may not have my children, I can cherish the rich patchwork of memories I have from their childhoods.

As I write, I know that Lucas's baby tooth is in the bottom of my desk, where it has been since the tooth fairy collected it seven years ago. I have saved the children's first clothes with their lingering baby scent and snippets of curls from their first haircuts. I have kept scrapbooks documenting the lovely and funny things they have said—and some of their cranky notes telling me why they were upset with me.

My memories of Jasper, Lucas and Toby as little children are as alive to me now as they've ever been. As babies, I knew their tired signs, their hungry cries, how easy or hard it was to get them settled to sleep, who sucked their thumb or their fingers, their favourite toys, and just how many blankets they each liked to have. I knew their favourite foods, their favourite songs, their friends at school, and I knew the world they grew up in. And they, too, have memories of our unbroken connection from the moment they were born. Our house has walls of photographs and cases of photo albums, and I have hoarded chests full of their drawings, paintings and all sorts of other ephemera.

I have nothing from Abdul's or Ahad's childhood. Those things are a mystery to me. I can only guess what they were like as children and what their life in Afghanistan was like from what they have told me. Guessing, though, is not as tangible as smelling a baby blanket or having that pang of just *knowing* your baby.

The becoming of a family is not something that is declared, or made; it is something that grows, made up of repeated interactions and precious memories. At the time we make them, in the living of them, what do we remember and why? If only I could recall, now, all those precious moments that have been allowed to slip away. Day by day, things are changing in our family. It is only in retrospect that I can see that we were becoming a family—not the one that I imagined in my head, but a real one.

Ahad begins to interact more and he begins to smile more. Ahad and I cook passionfruit slice side-by-side in the kitchen.

We try to meet on Fridays for lunch at the mall because he is the only boy willing to look at shops with me, and he has the best sense of style. Rob and Ahad work together in the garden, removing trees and digging trenches. Ahad gently teases Toby, who he has a special fondness for, by calling him 'Tobicles', which always gets a reaction. In defiance of the curfew, Ahad, Abdul, Jasper and I go out on a night run along a country road together, all carrying our torches, and we almost trip over a wombat. Ahad has decided to join the Rural Fire Service, mentored by my sister, who has volunteered and protected our community for years, and we laugh when, dressed in his uniform, he acts the clown by putting out a candle in the living room. I watch Abdul and Ahad deep in conversation with my parents at family dinners, or looking after Rob's sister Alice on a family walk, and feel happy that we can also be an extended family here.

The two boys also have their lives outside our household. They have connected with other Afghan people through the mosque and through asylum seeker networks. I am very happy about this because culture is important. And they have made friends at school.

I have tried to remember all I can of their first days at school because I have learned from my own boys how important these moments are.

Abdul and Ahad go to different schools from each other: Abdul is required to attend the one chosen by immigration and Ahad goes to the one closest to home. Abdul takes his bike on his first day. In his backpack is a blank book, a pencil case, a map and a folder of all the English essays and worksheets he had done in Darwin. When he gets home that first night, he tells me that he got lost twice on the way, despite our trial ride of the eight kilometres the day before. He didn't arrive until 11.30 a.m. and the teachers scolded him for missing classes. He explained that didn't know how to read the map. The head English teacher said that he was in a different educational system now, and despite his essays from Darwin and his wish to be in the mainstream, Abdul has to join the English-as-a-second-language course (ESL). So Abdul, in front of his new teacher, threw the folder of all of his old work in the bin. For the rest of the day he says he didn't think about talking to the other kids that much because he was worrying about how to get home. Each time the teacher's back was turned, he studied his map. Despite all the map study, he got lost on the way home too.

Ahad starts at school a few days after Abdul. He takes his time in the morning to iron his long-sleeved shirt and pants, and he had his hair cut the weekend before. He smells nice. He takes his wallet, a pen and a small notebook; his backpack looks sagging and empty. Ahad smiles as he recounts his first day. He tells us that his English teacher described his look as 'sharp' and that some of the other kids invited him to Maccas for lunch.

New traditions have also begun to develop. 'Poo face' is one of them. It starts slyly at dinner with someone shooting a weird facial expression across the table. Some are quiet, faraway smiles; very subtle. Or they may raise eyebrows, puff up their cheeks or make their faces red and strained. There seems to be no other point to the poo-face game except to make the other person laugh, and with five teenage boys it results in the same hilarity as fart jokes.

These are the memories I am starting to collect of our life together before each of these boys move away and start their own lives. Meanwhile, Abdul's and Ahad's childhood is held safely in their mother's heart in Afghanistan.

xxxxxxx

I shared something precious with Zaynab, Ahad and Abdul's mother, and I wanted to reassure her that her boys were doing well. Hearing them talk about their mother, her sense of humour and her strength, the problems she had faced, made me sure I would like her. They spoke to her regularly, but I had to harangue them to set up a Skype session.

One day, after we had all been together for a month, Abdul and Ahad called me over to the computer. I was wearing a summer singlet and would have liked to cover up, but wasn't willing to jeopardise what I had been asking for for so long by insisting I change my clothes before meeting their mum. Besides, if the boys didn't seem to notice what I was wearing, then it must have been fine.

The woman on the screen was about my age, or possibly younger, with bright eyes and an endearing smile just like her sons. She was wearing many more clothes than I was, including a white headscarf, which she twisted, rearranged and rewrapped during our talk. She was sitting on a woven rug in a small room, and from time to time one small child or another would dart across the room, sit in her lap, or stand behind her and stare at the computer screen. The boys told me they were relatives' children. When I smiled and waved to these kids, they gave shy smiles back, or ran away and hid.

Zaynab and I couldn't talk directly because we did not share the same language so we used the boys, particularly Ahad, as our interpreter. I told her that her sons were doing fine, they were working hard at school and were no trouble. She told me that she was happy that they were with me and that she gave me permission to boss them around if they needed it. Giving the boys a comical warning glance, I smiled and told her that I would be delighted to. As with all mothers, we could warmly communicate far beyond those words the boys translated for us. As I watched Abdul and Ahad speak Hazaragi with their mother, I felt as if they were there on the other side of the screen with her. I knew what the boys really wanted was to jump in and hug her.

After Zaynab and I had finished talking, some male relatives appeared. This is when I really wished the boys had warned me about my clothes. Despite being in my own house in Australia, and not due to any behaviour on their part, I felt underdressed again, awkward and shy. They wanted to ask questions about how to get to Australia, what sort of visa they needed, and how they might get one. They thought I had some expertise in these matters, and I told them I didn't. They seemed desperate, and although I told them the chances were slim they still appeared to have hope. The men were polite and appreciative of the small amount I could offer.

One man asked if it would be interesting for me to go for a walk with him via his smartphone on his way to pick up a friend. Yes, I would love to! We walked through the yard, where there were piles of snow melting on the ground, past the bare branches of fruit trees, and entered a street lined either side with dusty grey walls of stone. We walked along, passing groups of men. Sometimes he hid the phone and I noticed that he carefully ensured no one saw me. We came to a T-intersection opening on to a busier road and on the opposite side was a mosque. There had not been any women on this side street, but in the distance I could see some, fully covered, carrying bags of shopping. Crouching on the ground outside the mosque was a man who seemed very relieved to see my guide. Abruptly the phone went blank and I was back on our lounge room floor in Canberra. I'd had no opportunity to ask any questions or use any other senses except what was on the grainy screen of the phone, but I felt like I'd had a quick trip to Afghanistan.

Chapter 29

WATCHING TELEVISION

I hoped that television could be an undemanding way we could settle down as a family to relax together: some cosiness, maybe snacks, tea and a shared experience. Abdul and Lucas were agreeable to watching a bit of 'teev' with me, especially if there was the offer of a back scratch, foot rub or head massage, which I'd use to entice them away from the internet and their phones so we could hang out. Toby went to bed early, Jasper played computer games instead and Ahad would often say he'd be 'down soon' but never was. I think that he may have had the same difficulties with television that Abdul did when he first moved in.

Someone who has witnessed real violence does not watch explosions or bloodshed for entertainment so I was careful choosing what we watched. Despite my best efforts at vetting, we were surprised by how much violence there was on television. Whenever this happened, I could see the adrenaline (the 'flight-or-fight' chemical) coursing through Abdul's system like electricity. He usually walked away, but if he stayed I sensed that he was unhappy and restless.

One evening I thought we could watch something sweet and chose *Babe*, a movie about a little piglet who wants to become a sheepdog. This time all the boys gathered around the lounge room to watch the trailer, which started with the pig saying how he had lost his whole family and how he didn't fit in anywhere. The pig is alone in the barn sobbing when a motherly sheepdog tells him that she'll take care of him until he can look after himself and invites him to snuggle in with her puppies.

Tears came to my eyes: this was way too close to the bone. I wasn't ready to watch this with Abdul or Ahad and I turned it off with the excuse it was 'too young'. I was also worried that they might think I had deliberately chosen the movie for its narrative.

Then there was another challenge. Late one night, Abdul joined me in the lounge room as I was watching a French drama, but he quickly made the excuse that he needed some tea. I couldn't work out why he hadn't returned from the kitchen, but then it occurred to me. Boobs! Until that night I had never really registered how frequently bare breasts and sex scenes occur on television, but this was a culture clash for a modest boy. Eventually Abdul perfected the art of the pillow over the face and asked me to tell him when it was finished, rather than miss out on the whole program. The pillow technique is probably useful for all teenagers watching television with older folks.

Then there was the television series *Sherlock*. I was pretty sure this wouldn't have any nudity. Abdul had popped off to the kitchen to make tea, and as the opening credits played it quickly dawned on me that this would not work either. The episode started with Dr Watson's military experiences in Afghanistan, violent gunfire and people getting blown up in a dusty market street. When Abdul returned with a tray laden with mugs, ready to start watching, I lied and said the program wasn't loading. Maybe I should have told him why, but me saying, 'I don't think you should watch this,' was getting frustrating for both of us.

To reduce the risk of such problems in those early days, we only watched movies that I had seen before. The old ones. Abdul has an amazing memory. After we watched *The Man from Snowy River*, he would loudly exclaim, 'I'm not a lad, I'm a man!' We watched *Picnic at Hanging Rock* and a few weeks later Abdul alarmed some fellow walkers in the bush by calling out 'Miranda! Miranda!' We watched *Muriel's Wedding* one night and everything was 'You're terrible, Muriel!' Abdul has a wicked sense of humour. One day, while standing in a lift packed with chubby businessmen types, he brightly exclaimed, 'I bought a Jeep!'

After the *Fury* incident in Darwin, I wanted to ensure the first time Abdul went out to the movies with us would be a delightful experience. After settling down with a big bag of popcorn, we watched a gentle Australian comedy drama, connecting with the rest of the audience in their tears and laughter. I don't think I could have made a better choice.

Chapter 30

FOOD

Each time I visited my grandparents as a child near the Georges River bushland in Oatley, I would peek into their cottage-shaped biscuit barrel. Not only did the tiny, multi-paned windows and doors bordered by climbing roses delight me, but Gran nearly always had treats in there. Usually they were my favourite—small, buttery chocolate morsels topped with a shiny chocolate glaze.

When I bake these biscuits today, memories of being with my grandparents rise up like the scent of baking and fill me with warmth. I can still see the floral wallpaper of the guestroom where each of my cousins, at one time or other, manufactured a headache just to have Gran tuck us into bed and gently place an embroidered hanky dotted with drops of Yardley English Lavender cologne on our foreheads.

Those afternoons I would lie nestled between the cool sheets and listen to my grandparents talk or, more often, my grandfather sing and gently tease my gran. After enough rest, I would often creep out to watch my grandfather tending his azaleas and magnolias wearing old gardening pants hoiked up with string and an old police shirt with the badges torn off. The garden always had the tang of blood and bone fertiliser and what he said was elephant poo from the zoo.

Son, son, come away from the elephant's bum!

Oops, too late. Dig him out!

When Ahad came to visit us that first time, I could not resist making my gran's biscuits with him. You see, these little brown morsels are called Afghans! My Australian boys had insisted on baking biscuits by themselves for some time. And while it might be a good thing that a thirteen-year-old boy knows how to make a ganache, I had long-missed the business of baking side-by-side with happy, and often very sticky, little kids. I thought that biscuit-making with Ahad would be a chance for us to engage in some cosy domesticity together.

With Ahad at my side in the kitchen, I introduced him to the world of baking. Beating the butter and sugar until it is fluffy and all the sugar is dissolved does take time, I explained, but it's worth it. Next you need to fold in the flour, cocoa and crushed cornflakes. It needs strong arms, but not too much mixing or the biccies will get too hard. Ahad, with his careful attention to detail, made biscuits much nicer than mine.

We put the last batch into the oven and sat down with a cup of tea until the scent of slightly burned chocolate summoned the rest of the boys.

'Wait! They have to cool,' I said, shooing sneaky hands away. 'And we need to add the topping.'

The secret to the shiny chocolate icing was constant stirring over heat. After we'd finished the last step, Ahad smiled as he picked off the hard clumps of icing under the cooling racks to nibble, and surveyed his success.

When he returned to Brisbane, I had posted him boxes of home-baked biscuits every two weeks. I wanted him to know I hadn't forgotten about him. It was a piece of homeliness and love that I could give him to share with the other unaccompanied refugee boys in his group house until the day he joined our table at home.

Our kitchen table is a long trestle bench that was passed on to us by my athletics club when they upgraded to plastic. It's simple pine and was made by someone in their garage about twenty years ago. The table is covered in scars from being carried in the back of a trailer to a cross-country run each month and burns from the gas-heated tea urns near which the runners gathered at the end of each race to discuss their adventures. When Ahad joined us, this table started to gather memories of the seven of us together.

From the moment when all the boys have returned from school until dinnertime, the whole family orbits around the kitchen because the boys need to eat and because I like being with them. For this reason, I have always made sure there is a couch in the kitchen so the kids can flop down in the heart of the house.

We have also made sure, as far as we could, that evening meals are eaten together as a family so we can share the simple pleasure of sitting around a table surrounded by loved ones and good food. Since the arrival of Abdul and Ahad, though, we hadn't always eaten at our second-hand table. With many more meals enjoyed sitting on the floor, Afghan style, we were all learning to get comfortable, stretching out our hamstrings, which were tight from sitting on chairs all our lives.

Over the years, it has evolved that Rob does the cooking for family dinners. He says the prepping and preparing of food after work is a relaxation for him—except when I pinch the veggies off the chopping board while he's working! Rob often cooks the dishes he remembers from his childhood, and this sturdy, simple Hungarian food is excellent for active, growing boys. While the kitchen brings us together, the food connects our biological boys to their Hungarian roots and introduces Abdul and Ahad to yet another new cuisine.

Rob's signature dish is the healthy Australian version of the famous Hungarian soup, goulash. Lean beef—it doesn't matter what cut—is sautéed in a pan with oil (the Hungarian way is with lard), along with generous amounts of garlic and onions until the flavour of the seared meat is released and the onions are golden and transparent. A handful of caraway seeds is then thrown in, together with carrots, potatoes and a rich stock. And paprika, of course, more than you would think wise. Goulash is served with *nokedli*, tiny dumplings made by dripping batter through a grater into boiling water. The *nokedli* not only gives some body to the soup but helps concentrate the flavour, too.

The boys Hungarian favourite is *lángos*, pronounced more like 'larngorsh'. Plate-sized discs of deep-fried yeasty dough are served brushed with salty garlic sauce and sprinkled with grated cheese. My favourite comfort food, though, is *rakott krumpli*—made by Rob, of course. Layers of sliced potato are interspersed with sliced hardboiled eggs and *csabai* circles (a spicy Hungarian sausage). The whole lot is then smothered with sour cream before it's put in the oven. Simple food— until it comes out of the oven steaming, and the starchy potato and creamy egg contrasts with the crunch of salty sausage and burned potato edges. It is the food equivalent of sitting by a fireplace wrapped in a warm blanket. Sadly, we didn't eat this when Abdul and Ahad moved in because *csabai*, made with pork, was off the menu.

There have been some other changes to our diet, one of them being the amount of tea our family drinks. During many afternoons and evenings, we now sit drinking cups of tea accompanied by a big spread of almonds, dates and sultanas. It warms my heart to see Abdul boiling milky tea over the fireplace and then, with the pot by his side, he will attend to his Maths or other studies. This tea habit has also endeared the boys to Jasper, who has started taking a thermos of earl grey to school. Tea with honey begins to be consumed in such quantities that Rob decides to get a beehive. His 'girls', as he likes to call them, are slow to produce at first, but we can see some mighty fine teas with honey in the future.

When Abdul and Ahad moved in with us, we started eating halal food. In general, most fresh healthy and nourishing food is halal, except for pork, alcohol and other intoxicating substances that are *haram*, meaning forbidden in Islamic law. There are also specific rules to do with the slaughter process for meat. I visited a halal grocer as much as I needed to, but most chicken in Australia is halal and we already ate a lot of fish and vegetarian meals. Kangaroo is hard to classify, so it was soon off the menu. Rob and I drink wine with some meals, but we stopped cooking food with wine or any other spirit when the boys were eating with us. I became very aware of foods that may use animal by-products, such as rennet to make cheese, and gelatine (including lollies), which would be considered haram.

When the boys arrived, many people wanted to welcome them into the community. In Abdul's first week we were at a friend's home and a bag of 'Bacon and Egg' flavoured chips was being passed around. When I saw Abdul reach out to take a handful I tried to discreetly divert the chips, but Abdul, misunderstanding my intentions, quickly grabbed hold of the bag. My hopes to be subtle were lost in the scramble around spilled chips. At least now he knows that bacon, ham, speck and pork are all the same name for pig.

Over time, we learned a little more of how to cook Afghan food, especially as Ahad, our teacher, was a very good cook. His rice, cooked in the Afghan way with plump long grains all perfectly separate and flavourful, is a masterpiece. Trying to remember how to do it each time is a challenge, as there are literally dozens of slightly different techniques. First you need good, long-grain rice; the closest we can get in Australia is basmati. The rice needs to be washed and rinsed well—at least three times to remove the starch from the outside of the grains. It is then soaked for at least an hour, though Ahad soaked it for three. The rice is covered with water and boiled.

When the heat is removed some of the water is taken out before a cloth is wrapped around the lid and the pot goes back on to cook. When Ahad makes rice alongside his 'tomatoey' rich, red goat curry, the result is a delicious feast.

Abdul likes to have Afghan chutney when breaking his fast at Ramadan, a spicy but refreshing blend of fresh mint, coriander, lemon juice, garlic, cumin and chillies. He would have this with bolani, or over a simple *shorwa*, a bean, potato and meat soup, with naan bread to dunk.

My heart was in my mouth when I watched Ahad and Abdul in the kitchen for the first time. They did without a chopping board, instead holding the vegetables in their hands while cutting them with a sharp knife. When I suggested they keep their fingers attached, they told me this is how their mum cuts vegetables because she doesn't have a chopping board, or even a table.

One night Abdul returned home with a big bag of walnuts in their shells.

'How are we going to eat them?' I asked. 'We don't have a nut cracker.'

'Why would you need a nutcracker? It's easy, just watch.'

Abdul held two walnuts in his fist and with a tiny squeeze the shell of one cracked and the nut inside came out whole.

We were all learning together and from each other. While we were introducing our Afghan sons to the Australian way of doing things, they were teaching us that there was more than one way to do something—and often it was a simpler way.

Chapter 31

FAITH

It was in early 2015, and the prime minister, Tony Abbott, had made a statement of 'Nope, nope, nope' to a humanitarian crisis. Australia had been asked by its Asian neighbours to help resettle a boatload of Rohingya refugees who had been fleeing savage violence and persecution and were now stranded, starving, off the coast of Myanmar.

Abdul and I were discussing this over a pot of tea, safely in our lounge room. In response to the horror of the situation and the destruction of our nation's international reputation, I expressed my rhetorical desire to do violence to our prime minister for his callous response.

Abdul paused and looked at me gravely. He spoke in a firm voice.

'Don't let him be your teacher.'

His words stopped me in my tracks. Abdul, who had been so cold-heartedly treated, and so badly harmed by this politician's callous policies, would not countenance even a verbal expression of violence against the man.

Abdul is my teacher. I wish more people were as humble, principled and peace-loving as him.

xxxxxxx

Some people in Australia may wonder what it has been like having two Muslim boys live with us. My short answer is that it's just the same as having any other two boys. But there is a long answer, too.

Despite our different religious backgrounds, we share a common understanding around the ethics of kindness, tolerance and generosity. Islam is part of who Abdul and Ahad are, and I can see how their faith has given them solace and strength because it reminds them of the goodness of people, even in their darkest hours. In my opinion, all religions come down to these basic rules: be kind to each other, do the best you can for others, be the most decent person you can be, and find the beauty and joy in life.

We don't talk religion much at home because I don't want Abdul and Ahad to think that my casual questions mean that Islam is a mere curiosity to me, or that they have to explain or prove themselves. I especially do not want them to think my asking is questioning the validity of their beliefs—there is enough anti-Islamic attitude around in Australia without them worrying about this at home. Abdul's and Ahad's spiritual welfare is important to all of us in their Australian family.

Our first, and probably only, bump over religion, came around Ramadan in June 2015. By this time, Abdul had been living with us for a little over six months and Ahad for four. The holy month for Muslims, Ramadan is a time for reflection, prayer, charity and goodness to others. It also means fasting, a time when Muslims must not eat or drink between sunrise and sunset. Ramadan means restraint: controlling one's temper and practising patience and peacefulness, which can be a challenge with low blood sugar. Ramadan is difficult for the believer; it is meant to be, but it is also meant to be approached with equanimity and pleasure.

I thought that the first Ramadan would be even more of a challenge for Abdul and Ahad since they were living with a non-Muslim family in Australia. The rest of us, especially their Australian teenage brothers, ate almost around the clock, as did most of the general community. School exams and sports training continued, along with just about everything else, not taking fasting into consideration. We tried to make it as easy as we could for Abdul and Ahad, sometimes guessing what was needed as we went along. Dates and snacks were ready each evening to break their fast, and Rob and I also tried, as much as possible with our busy schedules, to have dinner ready early for those 30 days.

I am guessing many Muslim parents—even in Afghanistan—need to give their growing adolescent boys a little nudge as a reminder to be pleasant and kind in their interactions with the rest of the family. But at times Abdul and Ahad, perhaps understandably, took my consternation at them being grumpy as being disparaging of their fasting and their religion. But their Muslim faith is part of who they are and I respect and admire that these boys are so observant during Ramadan. They are good people; they are both kind and patient, and this helped all of us get through the difficult patches.

Chapter 32

MAGIC CARPETS

We have a small and humble Persian carpet in our house. Nestled into its worn and faded red background are the most beautiful bright-blue and yellow flowers and birds. When the boys were little, they all loved to sit on it as Rob told them his magic flying carpet stories. Mysteriously, the stories always happened to three little boys, who also happened to have the same names as our boys, but in the 'magic carpet world' they had switched ages. Sometimes, if the carpet went too fast in their imagination, the two eldest would hold tight to either side of the rug while baby Toby sat content in Rob's lap. The stories always ended with the three of them zooming away to their next adventure, snuggled together in the safety of their daddy and the carpet.

At the same time Rob was telling bedtime stories, 11,000 kilometres away on the other side of the world Ahad and Abdul had also been young children, but their world was very different. While my boys were playing in their nice, warm house with their imaginary stories on their magic carpet, Ahad and Abdul were making carpets for twelve to fourteen hours a day.

Because of attacks by heavily armed gangs, the family had fled their village in Hazarajat. With no land to farm and no home, they worked side-by-side each day weaving carpets to eke out enough money to live by. Abdul told me with great pride that he was put in charge of making the flower patterns on the carpets, and sometimes embroidery around the little round mirrors that adorn clothing and other textiles, because his small hands were more dextrous than the adults.

I heard this story one evening as we were sitting on our tiny carpet eating a pre-dinner snack of biscuits and soft cheese. When Ahad started laughing, I asked him why. The small mound of cheese we were casually eating, he said, was about the same amount of food they had to eat as a family of seven when they were carpet-weaving. He took another mouthful with a huge grin on his face.

This family had not fled their land and mountain village to escape poverty. If it had been safe to stay in their home, they too could have had enough to eat—as farming families had for generations before—and Abdul and Ahad could have remained sitting on their carpets with their parents and lived as children should, in a world of safety, imagination and play. Their family fled because their lives were in danger and their poverty was a result of this need to flee. In the same way, Abdul and Ahad also did not flee to Australia because of the family's poverty. They fled because they weren't safe, and what they were forced to leave behind were the most precious things in the world to them.

Chapter 33

FAMILY PRIDE

A teacher one day asked me what my boys thought about Abdul and Ahad moving in with us. He had known of other families doing something similar where the kids were not so thrilled to have new 'family members'. There was no simple answer, of course, and this is what I told him.

It isn't always easy to have extra people in the household, and sometimes it's hard for children to understand why their parents would make such a decision. From the beginning, of course, I agonised about the impact my choices would have on my boys because their welfare counts more than anything else. Unlike Abdul and Ahad, they have only one family and we are it.

For all mums and dads, parenting is an ongoing risk-management exercise. We only ever get one chance with our kids' childhoods; there is no rewind button if you stuff it up.

Having Abdul and Ahad move in with us was a risk, and Rob and I had our fair share of 'tut-tut' warnings from others about not trusting Muslims and the risks of having two traumatised teenagers from a violent, war-torn country living under our roof. But these boys were not strangers to me when I invited them into our home and I always knew Abdul and Ahad were gentle souls. Rob and I are not stupid, nor are we naïve or cavalier about the safety and health of our family. We went in with our eyes open.

Instead of seeing only risks, we saw having Abdul and Ahad join us as enriching all our lives. We wanted our children to see the big picture of life and that ethics are not just a mouthing of intentions but *doing*—and that often the doing is hard. Of course, none of us could have fully predicted what life would be like when these Afghan boys moved in. What I most worried about was that my children would feel displaced and believe that I was more interested in these new additions to the family, or that my love for them had been diluted. This has not been the case: the more slices of love I have given, the more I have left, just like the magic pudding. And it seems that helping the Afghan boys, and being needed by them, has helped me better manage those moments of sadness that are sparked when I see my Australian boys growing up and wanting more independence.

When I first proposed that Abdul come to stay with us, my eldest son, Jasper, asked the entirely appropriate question, 'What if he's a dickhead?' But because his sense of humour has always been so perceptive and mocking of the cruelty in the asylum seeker debate, he added, 'Well, we can always get immigration to send him back.' And yet he has been more gracious than I could expect any teenage boy to be. Jasper has worked steadily from the ground up in growing his relationship with Abdul and Ahad. Watching Jasper and Abdul sitting side-by-side quietly working out a puzzle together, or making electronic circuits, fills my heart.

Lucas is more forthright in his opinions, asking questions and expressing his feelings. This is not only courageous but healthy. It can't have been easy for a twelve year old to make these big adjustments. The same year he transitioned to high school and became a teenager these two older boys moved in and took up a lot of his mother's time and emotional energy. Although his remarks and arguments might end up cutting too close to the bone, his humour often makes him the family circuit-breaker. I love the way Lucas was simply himself right away with Abdul and Ahad.

Toby embraced his new brothers with a sense of fun and adventure, and he and the boys have created a beautiful bond. He has been so interested in all they have to tell him, and I think he has learned enough to fit right into an Afghan village pretty quickly now, though I am not sure acquiring every rude word in Hazaragi is entirely useful unless he is fluent in the rest of the language . . . It is delightful to hear loud laughs and an occasional thud emanating from the lounge room because it means Toby and Abdul are engaged in yet another play-wrestling match. When I see the joyful affection between them, I know how devastated Toby would be if Abdul was ever taken away.

And, yes, there have been problems. Everyone in the

family has needed time to adjust. When Abdul and Ahad first arrived, all three of my Australian boys became distracted at school. It was an anxious time for this mother bird, but I hoped—and it has proven true—that, like baby birds learning to fly, they would drop down a little to work out where they were in the world until the wind caught their wings again.

The foundations of family everywhere in the world are connection and love, but there are cultural differences affecting how these things evolve. Coming from Afghanistan, a country with no welfare system and where many families survive on subsistence agriculture, strongly defined family roles and hierarchies are essential for survival. In their culture, the boys were not just joining a family, they were taking on lifetime responsibilities. And so, for Abdul and Ahad, the decision to join our family was not taken lightly. I think this attitude made it simpler for our Afghan boys to decide that our family was theirs. For my Australian boys, and also for Rob, the process was a more gradual one of getting to know Abdul and Ahad before accepting them as family. This difference led to some unhappiness when the Afghan boys saw that my sons were not as keen to immediately accept their role as brothers in the way they thought they should.

I remember a day when Lucas, who was feeling distressed after witnessing me struggling to communicate with Abdul and Ahad, blurted out to them, 'Well, what are you even doing here?' Lucas had been dealing with some big changes and unasked-for disruptions to his family. But I also understood why this upset Abdul and Ahad, who took this outburst as evidence of still not being accepted into the family.

I explained to Abdul and Ahad that it takes time to build a brotherly relationship from the ground up. I tried to understand why sometimes, perhaps from their cultural viewpoint, it has been hard for them to understand my Australian boys' behaviour. It has always been important to me that Abdul and Ahad know that their Australian brothers care about them, even though they may not show it all the time. They are, after all, teenage boys living together.

I am proud of our Australian boys, and although they are not perfect—I think perfect is a bit weird—they have been the most gracious and accepting kids I think our Afghan boys could have met. Like the time one evening when Abdul arrived home unexpectedly just as the rest of us had all sat down to a roast-chicken dinner. As Abdul went upstairs to change, the family, as one and with no hesitation, filled Abdul's plate with roast chicken and potatoes and peas from their own plates.

I love the family culture of silliness the boys have created together. Recognising each other's hare-brained teenage-boy antics, such as catching farts in syringes and chasing each other around the house, laughing hilariously. Why would you even *do* that?

To Jasper, Lucas and Toby, I love you boys, fiercely, and with everything I have, and more than you could ever know until you become parents yourselves. The way you have accepted Abdul and Ahad into our family is a testament to your kindness and equanimity. You are all kind, generous and resilient people. I admire you and am so proud of you. You three are my heroes.

Chapter 34

GROWING PAINS

Abdul and Ahad tried very hard to adapt to our family too. Of course there were things that didn't go smoothly, and as a parental figure I occasionally had to go toe-to-toe with these adolescent Afghan boys. Most of the time the issue was about chores, a subject that drove me spare. I acknowledge that, if I asked them, Ahad and Abdul would work very hard at jobs alongside me, but I found it incomprehensible that they simply would not take on a small, regular chore around the home to help lighten my load.

Officially, all the boys had delegated jobs, but Ahad only occasionally did his, which was scooping leaves out of the pool, while Abdul's weekly sweep of the courtyard has, to date, happened twice. The other three mostly did their chores, but it was strictly 'work to rule' for them and nothing more. All five boys were leaving the burden of work around the house to Rob and me.

Apart from the fact we worked full-time, Rob and I believed chores were important for each member of a family because they were a sign of joint responsibility and teamwork. Chores also relieved the burden of continual delegation: remembering and asking is a job in itself. Needing to ask in the 'right way' and waiting to ask at the 'right time' can make hard work out of what should have been straightforward responsibilities for teenagers. For example, if my tone of voice was not right, or if someone was in the middle of homework/resting/ watching television/computer games/eating, they considered this enough of an excuse to put it off. Or, if the job was grudgingly accepted but then not done, my reminder of the chore could cause a whole new drama in itself!

I remember my disgust when working in Adelaide in the late nineties. I was called to see a mentally unwell Afghan man who had been fixing carpets for no pay other than the 'privilege' of some food and sleeping in a dirty garage. In trying to understand what I saw as Abdul's and Ahad's reluctance to help, I wondered if they thought they were being used as some type of indentured labour. I was pretty sure, though, that these twenty-minute-a-week jobs with me were not exploitation.

It crossed my mind that perhaps they thought helping around the house was women's work, but deep down I knew that this wasn't the case either. Rob was more laidback about chores than me, and with the new older boys he was polite but hands-off, leaving the 'parenting' to me.

Sometimes our misunderstandings over the chores issue became inflamed and turned into arguments, with Abdul and Ahad snapping back that I was deliberately picking fights because I'd had a bad day at work or to show them that I had all the power. On this issue, they pushed back hard and I did too, but, really, it was related to all of us feeling vulnerable.

Abdul and Ahad tried hard to manage their homesickness and sadness, and my heart was feeling it with them. Their emotional turmoil when they heard news of more terror in Afghanistan, and their quieter moments of sadness when they were missing family and home, especially their mother, was tough. The boys seldom acknowledged it, let alone talked about it. On the worst days, I felt like I had been blind-folded on a roller-coaster: I had gut-wrenching sensations of emotions but no idea of what was happening or when this awful ride would stop.

The trouble was that when the Afghan boys were strug-gling with their unexpressed emotions I sometimes failed to recognise the signs that they were not coping. I lumped their emotional withdrawal, which I called their 'checking out', with their not helping with chores—and in my tired state of mind saw both as an indication they just didn't care. In fact, there were times in those early months when all five boys were not coping.

My Australian boys' school grades dropped the first semester Abdul and Ahad lived with us. But what really dis-tressed me was how my boys had become super picky and mean to each other. The same type of thing had happened some years before when we moved our family to Canada, so I hoped that this was also a temporary response to change and that we would all bounce back.

I noticed that our boys were careful not to show their irritations to the new kids, but between themselves the sibling rivalry increased. This was usually played out with Jasper, the oldest, totally ignoring his brothers' presence. Lucas, who has a superhuman power to bait his brothers, would react to these snubs with a carefully intoned but intentionally irritating 'Good morning, Jasper.' Or Toby, the youngest, would simply fly off the handle.

If the disputes between my boys had been more explicit, it might have been easier to step in, but because each slight was so deliberately under the radar the tensions became like a slow-burning poison in the home. I tried all I could to give each of them more of my time, but, being teenage boys, there was only so much time they wanted to spend with me. It was a horrible situation and I had no idea what to do. I had five teenage boys who all needed me, patients to see each day, hospital rounds to do in the evening and, lastly, my marriage to look after.

All of this was quietly sucking the life out of what Rob and I had together. And yet I knew it was me who had pushed to have these boys with us and so I felt it was my responsibility to do the hard yards. I had a fear that if I told Rob how difficult it was for me he might not understand and say Abdul and Ahad should leave. We both knew we were stressed, but as doctors, and as endurance athletes, we kept on pushing back our own time together in order to get the job done.

So many nights I didn't sleep at all. At some point I started grinding my jaw and cracked through one of my front teeth. Some days I was so fatigued I felt like I couldn't move. I was frustrated with the boys, but at the same time, when I saw they were struggling, I struggled with them. We were all on this roller-coaster together. My clinical brain told me I wasn't really depressed. It was an adjustment.

There was something primitive and obsessive in my feelings towards Abdul and Ahad. As a psychiatrist who saw new mothers and babies, I recognised my feelings and behaviour were similar to the postnatal adjustment that nearly all mothers experience in the first few months after birth—the state of 'primary maternal preoccupation'. This phrase was coined by Donald Winnicott, one of the first psychoanalysts to consider the real-life interactions of infants and their mothers.

He argued that it is normal and necessary for a mother to become completely obsessed by her new baby. For an utterly dependent newborn, a mother's absolute focus on their needs is required for their survival, but in most other circumstances these behaviours would be regarded as unhinged. Research has found that a neurotransmitter hormone, oxytocin, is probably responsible for fuelling this mental state. Released by the pituitary gland of the brain, it is what makes mothers' milk flow. It is also involved in falling in love and the psychiatric condition of obsessive-compulsive disorder.

Through the physical and biological processes of holding and soothing their babies, feeding them and seeing them grow stronger, new mothers have the chance to settle the fevered obsessionality of primary maternal preoccupation. Once reassured that their babies will survive, they can relax.

The process of falling in love with our babies—making a place in our hearts for loving a new person—sometimes hurts. Maybe our heart tears a little to let this new love in. Because new mums are so wonderfully focused on their child's every feeling, they can become more sensitive to everything else. This can evoke memories and emotions of what it was like for them when they were themselves babies and, sadly, sometimes these may not always be happy. Confronting these emotions while filling our heart with the love for our babies is part of the bravery of motherhood.

I did not expect this love to be how it was—I expected something more clinical, more distant and objective. 'Fat chance,' fate told me. In the beginning, I had a fevered need to hold on to my new boys. Literally hold on. Not just because I wanted to take away all the hurt and separation they had been through, but because I could feel my heart and brain adapting like a new mother. And yet it was perplexing as they were not my babies at all: they were teenage boys with their own mother, and soon I would need to let them go into the world because these boys were almost men.

Many months after Abdul and Ahad came to live with us, they told me why they had to leave Afghanistan. I am not at liberty to tell this part of their story. What I can say is that it was harrowing, and as I listened a cold fear and darkness gripped the back of my neck. I recognised that spectre; I have seen it as patients relive their traumas in my office. That type of horror never leaves a person: it can only be managed.

I knew that the world for them had not been safe, but still I wanted to make it better. I knew I couldn't take away what they had been through. I can't ever make up for the lost years Ahad has suffered and I couldn't protect Abdul from the overhanging threat that immigration could take him away from us at any time.

Chapter 35

AHAD THE STOUT-HEARTED

Soon after I met Ahad, he asked me what Australian name he should adopt once he got his citizenship. He thought it would make it easier to fit in. The first thing I told him was that he shouldn't have to change his name as it is part of who he is. On the other hand, I also knew the reality: that an Anglo-sounding name can open more doors. My father-in-law, Sándor, did the same in order to assimilate when he first arrived in Australia. And sadly, even now, it seems that not a great deal has changed: several studies have found that non-Anglo sounding names can negatively affect potential employers' attitudes. Although I didn't know Ahad well enough to offer a suggestion, a name that came to mind was Sam. After Sam Gamgee, from Tolkien's saga: quiet and unassuming, stout-hearted, devoted and conscientious. This was Ahad.

Ahad took his role in our family very seriously and was protective of me. Whenever we walked down the street together, he was always on his guard, although I think his hyper-vigilance was also likely due to shadows of his experiences. Such a weight for a young man to carry.

Ahad told me about his escape from Afghanistan several months after he moved in and since then he has said no more about it. We had just been on a long run and were walking back through town side by side. If an observer took at face value the unemotional and disconnected way Ahad told his story, they might have thought it was nothing more than a simple explanation of travelling from A to B. Except it wasn't. Ahad's escape from Afghanistan was horrific and a matter of life and death; many others who fled when he did died.

After saying goodbye to his family, possibly for the last time, Ahad took a bus alone from Kabul to Kandahar. He told me that this bus was going too fast, the driver was probably drunk, and people were screaming at him to slow down. The bus rolled, killing many of the passengers. Ahad, who was around thirteen at the time, thinks he saw about 25 bodies.

From Kandahar, he was transported to Malaysia. These unaccompanied children never know what route they will be made to take; during each leg of the journey they are kept in the dark until the last minute, and they are at the absolute mercy of the people smugglers. When they arrived in Malaysia, they drove through the jungle with Ahad stuffed in the boot of a car for hours, so tightly packed in he couldn't move. He told me he suffered burns to his backside from the hot metal as a result.

When they arrived on the coast, the asylum seekers were herded on to a fishing boat to negotiate the Straits of Malacca into Indonesia. The Straits is one of the most dangerous shipping routes in the world, beset with tropical storms, crowded shipping lanes, floating rubbish and pirates. On the first night, the boat's engine failed, leaving the boat adrift. As the ocean became higher, big waves crashed in, and there was nothing that could be done. For hours, Ahad and the others on board, including small children, were pummelled in the dark. With the captain in tears, and with no one able to swim, everyone believed they were going to die. All they could do was hold each other and pray. Eventually, a mobile signal sent help to the people smugglers, and in the dark, rough seas the human cargo was transferred into another boat that eventually reached land.

Once in Indonesia, there was another journey in a car racing through the jungle and yet another motor vehicle accident. This time Ahad broke his ankle, but he couldn't allow this to stop him as he had to run and hide. As he told me this part, he joked about the biting insects, but all I could think about was that he couldn't abide frogs and snakes, and there would have been plenty of those in the jungle. Or perhaps that is why. Ahad was captured by the police and put in jail. Indonesia is not a signatory to the UN Refugee Convention and this is how they treat asylum seekers. Remarkably, he escaped. In an episode worthy of its own movie, Ahad managed to climb a wall with a broken ankle and hide in the jungle again.

Ahad paused in his storytelling there and stopped walking for a bit. I don't think he wanted to dwell on it. We walked in silence, except for the scuffling and crunching of autumn acorns scattered over the path. After a few more blocks, Ahad continued. Though his last boat had almost sunk in the Straits of Malacca, coupled with the fact that he couldn't swim, Ahad left Indonesia via the sea, spending three long days on another crowded fishing boat. When he saw the Australian Navy on the water, Ahad told me, 'I thought I was born again.' But his journey wasn't over. Instead he was locked up on Christmas Island and then in Darwin for five months before finally being set adrift in Brisbane.

When Ahad moved in with us at the end of that summer of 2015, I wasn't aware that he couldn't swim. It was only when I observed his unwillingness to jump into the river with us one hot afternoon that I realised he could barely dog paddle. It brought on an anxiety I hadn't experienced since my boys were small. Not being able to swim is dangerous, and living in Australia, with all our beautiful water, makes this a big social handicap.

So I taught Ahad how to swim.

We started in our shallow backyard pool. Every day I helped Ahad work up from the basics, getting a good technique in kicking, keeping his body aligned and his head down. Abdul, who had taught himself to swim while in detention, came to some of these sessions to cheer his brother on. We moved to the indoor Olympic pool nearby and in that tiled echo chamber he swam lap after lap until swimming practice became more like a training regime. In only a few months Ahad developed a graceful and efficient freestyle, breaststroke and sidestroke. To make use of his conscientious and protective instincts, I suggested that he should get a life-saving certificate. Over the next few months, Ahad completed the relevant Royal Life Saving Society training courses and tests and is now a qualified pool lifeguard.

When Ahad first moved in with us, he had transferred schools to finish Year Twelve in Canberra. During his first months at school in Canberra, Ahad worked hard and his teachers gave unanimous feedback about a popular, polite and conscientious student. I was so proud of this young man who had so much potential. When Ahad smiled, his warmth and kindness shone through.

School was still hard for Ahad. His education in Afghanistan had been basic, but at least he had learned how to read Dari. Being literate in one's own language is a good foundation for learning another. As a shy young kid, he had spent five months in the same detention centre in Darwin as Abdul later did, before being moved to the group house in Brisbane, where survival was more of a priority than learning. All this meant that Ahad missed the chance of English immersion at an earlier age, which could have helped so much. His English was improving quickly, but due to those years of relative isolation as an unaccompanied minor it was still difficult.

In Canberra, Ahad found it hard to concentrate at school. Every day his worries increased when hearing news about what was happening in Afghanistan. He was anxious about his family, who were still facing threats, but most distracting were the flashbacks and dissociation. Flashes of images, of smells, of sounds of the horrors he had witnessed in Afghanistan would flood over him as he sat at his desk, while waves of fear and sadness would distract him from Maths or an English essay. Ahad told me that his mind would just switch off and he would suddenly not be there. Ahad is an intelligent person and having one's mind not let you think in a straight line must have been incredibly frustrating.

Ahad was simply not able to give his schoolwork the attention it needed and I was too tired to see how hard he was working to just manage. He hid his pain well. He was also taking too much responsibility for my feelings.

When we went through a bad patch, rather than him seeing my struggles as what they were—a tired mum looking after the needs of five teenage boys—he took it personally. Despite my denials, he insisted that he and Abdul were the cause of my sadness when in truth what I wanted was connection and perhaps a more tangible indication of gratitude.

Then, one night in winter after an argument that got too heated for its own good, Ahad left, booking a flight to Brisbane for the next day and slamming the door on the way out.

How I wish we could have had more time and space, and maybe someone who could have helped us both see the bigger picture. I know that we both wanted things to work out, but I just didn't know how to make it happen.

xxxxxxx

It was a sickening feeling. Like flying a kite when you think the string is tethered but instead of feeling a tug at the end of the line . . . suddenly there is nothing. This kite had been torn and battered and the thread had frayed. I tried to help. I held on hoping my efforts and my love could provide some bearings. I tried to make a safe haven. There were moments that the kite was able to fly and dance freely in the wind. But storms have been ever-present, whipping and shaking this kite, threatening to pull it from the sky. I held on; I did not let go, though my hands bled, my heart burned and my eyes filled with tears.

Chapter 36

A MOMENT OF DELIGHT

A had had only been with us for six months when he returned to live with the young Hazara men in Brisbane. After he moved out, Abdul, Toby and I started travelling to Brisbane to see him, or flew him back to Canberra so all the boys could be together.

Abdul and Ahad had an uncle and aunt who had immigrated to Australia many years before the boys, and on our first trip to Brisbane we were invited to lunch in their lovely home. It was a pleasure to sit on the beautiful cushions and the enormous matching handmade rugs in their sunny front room. I also couldn't help noticing the pride and care that had been taken in housekeeping, along with the exquisite small details, such as the beading on the pale, gauzy curtains and the ornaments from Afghanistan in the dustless white melamine display case. The house was so scrupulously clean and the garden so neat that I was in wonder at how this could be a household swarming with children from their twenties down to nursery age.

That day I was nursing a cold, trying to keep the misery of my blocked nose and fever to myself. Ahad had not yet arrived from work and Abdul was busy eating, yacking and catching up with everyone. Toby, who had kept me company for a while until he got into the groove with some of the boys who were near his age, left me to sit quietly with my thoughts.

Some of the older cousins, who were now at university, chatted with me in their broad ocker accents, but I was disappointed not to be able to converse with Ahad's aunt in English. I would have been delighted to share stories about her nephews. The aunt took herself and the girls away to the kitchen to prepare the food. With them gone, I felt awkward at being the only female in the room, though I didn't feel I could descend uninvited into the kitchen, especially with my sneezing and spluttering attacks. I was relieved when she sat down beside me after lunch. Abdul had finally stopped eating and began translating for us.

At one point, she handed me a phone to show me a video of a Hazara wedding that had taken place in Australia about a year earlier. As the camera panned over the wedding guests, I saw ladies in colourful dresses with dramatic eyes done with kohl, false eyelashes and iridescent eye shadow. The men were wearing white billowy pants and traditional long, white shirts, some with beautiful embroidery on the chest, others with handsomely embroidered vests. I could faintly hear the music underneath the noise of people talking and laughing as the camera showed women and men dancing in separate groups. Nearly everything was unfamiliar to me until I saw Ahad and my heart beat harder with recognition. He looked so handsome wearing his Afghan pants and long top, his *koti* waistcoat and embroidered Hazaragi cap. People had gathered around and cheered enthusiastically as he danced solo in the middle of the room. What a revelation! I knew this Ahad was in there, but I'd never seen this exuberance or talent before.

Abdul explained that Ahad was doing a *qataghani* dance, which means something along the lines of silly, wild or happy. No one could deny it was beautiful. Starting with small, springing steps to the music—one foot pointing one way and then the other—Ahad held his arms out to the side and then they rose above his head. This was definitely a masculine dance, with his shoulders and chest leading the way. His shoulders danced with shrugging movements and his hands gestured elegantly. As he ducked and twirled, Ahad's face was alight. He owned this dance, and the audience showed him their animated appreciation. Ahad looked happy and connected: his body was alive and his eyes were radiant. I caught a glimpse of his soul that day and it was beautiful.

xxxxxxx

After he left our home, Ahad still messaged me occasionally, but I didn't hear what was really going on for him unless Abdul told me. When I heard that Ahad had got an apprenticeship as a painter I was so relieved. It's a good trade, and it is a job where, if needed, one can be alone with one's thoughts.

But then I heard he stopped his apprenticeship because he felt he could earn more as a labourer and then I heard he was working too hard—all the hours he could get—and that he had stopped going to the gym because he was too tired. The news kept piling up. He had lost weight; Ahad was skinny now. There were no English classes and he had very little social life.

I know Ahad felt the burden of responsibility for his family in Afghanistan and the need to work every hour he could. He was also working himself to the bone to show the Australian government that he could support his family if they ever got here. I am sure this was not what Zaynab had intended when she sent her boys away. Freedom is not an endless cycle of physical labour to the edge of breaking and being too tired to do anything else. In Canberra, we had conversations about 'investing' in education, like undertaking some TAFE courses, because he had a marvellous business idea and all he needed was the energy and the certificates.

Then I heard he had collapsed at work. The doctor told him he had a heart murmur and he had to have an echocardiogram (an ultrasound of the heart to see how all the pumps and valves work). Ahad thought he was going to die.

Eventually, when Abdul told me about his brother's health, I called Ahad and I persuaded him to show me the echocardiogram report. His heart was okay. The murmur was not a problematic one. What caused the collapse was him working too hard and not eating enough. I pleaded with Ahad to slow down and take the time to rest. I told him that I was proud of his hard work but I was worried he was doing too much.

There was little response to this, but he did send thanks when I posted him a grocery delivery of healthy snacks, nuts and milk drinks.

The scan may have been clear, but I worried that this young man's heart had been weighed down for too long.

Chapter 37

RUNNING

When I first visited Abdul at Blaydin detention centre, one of our early conversations had been about running. Abdul was born in Hazarajat near the Koh-i-Baba mountains, the western arm of the great Hindu Kush mountain range. Abdul told me how he later ran up the mountains surrounding his home in Kabul. When I researched Kabul and surrounds on Google Maps, I saw intimidating steep slopes of rocks and scree. As a runner, I was impressed.

Abdul told me of the time when he convinced his friends to set out with him at 3 a.m. for an adventure up the mountain. They grasped one another's hands and tied their scarves together so as not to slip down the rock face. Towards the evening, and after many hours, he led the boys back down the mountain. His friends' energy was flagging because they'd run out of food, so Abdul scrounged some from people picnicking nearby. In this adventure story, I recognised a kindred spirit.

Despite all the time that Abdul had spent in a small compound in sweltering Darwin, he surprised me soon after his arrival in Canberra by running up the 250-metre rocky ascent to the top of Black Mountain without stopping. As he regained his fitness, we planned longer adventures, but during those first few weeks we stuck to training runs around the bush near our home, or running intervals on the athletics track. When Ahad, who was regarded as the 'runner' of his family, came to live with us, he would come too, though at that time his main focus was the gym.

In a relatively short period, Abdul's running became exceptionally good, especially on the hard, technical trails, which came as no surprise considering his life in the mountains. Abdul and Ahad are both like mountain goats, so perhaps it is in the blood? When we were running downhill together, I always told them to go first so I wouldn't hold them up, but really it was so I could marvel at how they danced down the rocky trails.

xxxxxx

In August 2015, and maybe as a distraction now Ahad had left, Abdul and I entered a 25-kilometre mountain race. For us, it was simply a chance to do some sightseeing and to run somewhere new, but after Abdul blitzed the field he was talent-spotted and there was a clamour from the organisers to find him a coach so he could train with other elite runners.

In the end, Abdul decided that he had enough to worry about without the pressure of serious training and competition. Running would continue to be about adventures and fun.

Running together gave us the time and opportunity to bond, but it also gave us the chance to discover new places and share new experiences. Initially we went all over Canberra, but after immigration allowed Abdul to stay out overnight we could explore further afield. In NSW, we ran in the Southern Highlands, the Northern Tablelands, the South Coast, Sydney, the Blue Mountains and Mount Canobolas near Orange. In Queensland, we ran in Brisbane, the Gold Coast hinterland and Far North Queensland. In fact, everywhere we have gone together, we have also run together.

By running with Abdul, I have had the joy of watching this boy connect with and develop a love for the Australian bush. There have been so many beautiful places that we would never have discovered, including Monga National Park on the escarpment between Canberra and the coast, which has become our special place. Here are hidden places of magic. Even on the hottest days of summer Monga's forests are shady and cool, and the clean rush of the Mongarlowe River revives our tired legs. In autumn, the rare native plumwoods cover the ground with scented petals as if a faerie wedding had just passed by. In winter, the tall ribbon gums and bowers of tree ferns veiled with mist make it an otherworldly experience.

No matter where we are, wildlife abounds when we run in the bush. Maybe the animals don't see us as a threat, or perhaps we sneak up on them too quickly. We've almost tripped over wombats in the evenings, seen lyrebirds, possums, echidnas, lizards, our fair share of snakes and, of course, oodles of kangaroos and wallabies.

Running is good for our bodies and our spirits. It can quieten our upset feelings, lighten our mood and boost our capacity to deal with stress. Running also provides the best time for talking. Our conversations can range from the profound to the silly. Usually we talk, often we laugh, and sometimes we sing! Running also helps regulate sleep. When I find that Abdul has been out running again at 2 a.m. because of nightmares, I no longer worry about the risks. Instead I am glad that Abdul has discovered running is a safe haven. I am also glad it is something we can share.

Chapter 38

ID TAGS

The afternoon before a trail running race in the Southern Highlands of NSW, Abdul and I went for a walk through Bundanoon National Park. It was early spring and soft yellow wattles, red bottlebrush sprays, white tea-tree blossoms and banksias were in flower. An occasional waft of a citrus-rose told me that the pink star-shaped boronia flowers were somewhere, but, as usual, not to be easily found. The path crunched underfoot as we descended from the sandstone plateau. As we got closer to the falls, the sound of rushing water became louder and in a shady, mossy gully we jumped across a small stream that had carved its course through the rock.

'I'm glad there aren't any crocodiles here.'

I thought this was an odd comment from Abdul. We walked on to the waterfall. Walking with teenage boys helps conversations start, but it works better to wait for them to continue rather than interrupt with questions.

We sat on some boulders and watched the water tumble a hundred or so metres down the rock face to a river hidden in the forest below. Having prepared well for his race the next day, Abdul was thinking about running.

'Many times in Blaydin I thought about running away,' he said. 'But it wasn't the wire fence that stopped me.'

The detention centre was surrounded by a swamp—where there definitely *are* crocodiles—and it was also a hot, dusty and exposed 40 kilometres from town. Abdul told me that he challenged the guards, telling them that if he decided to leave there was nothing they could do to stop him. After these conversations, the guards would discourage him from exercising and give grisly warnings about crocodiles, sharks and snakes. His counselling sessions were also increased.

Other boys had escaped, he told me, but they'd been caught and brought back a few months later. 'They made it not good for them,' he said.

We sat in quietness until a squabble of tiny golden whistler birds brought us back to the present and we heaved ourselves off the rocks to continue down the escarpment. The eucalyptus trees became taller as we moved downhill, where the smaller spiky grass trees gave way to tree ferns whose lacy canopies filtered the light. The ground became springy and moist with a thick layer of leaves and mushroom-scented rotting wood. Climbing down some rocky steps, Abdul turned back to me.

'What is sexual abuse?' he asked.

Startled by the question, I pretended that negotiating the rocks was a little tricky, while ugly scenarios rushed through my head. An unaccompanied child . . . a refugee . . . by himself thousands of kilometres from friends and family . . . vulnerable. Bad things happen to children during their flight. I'd also seen how easily people were abused at detention centres. I was scared of what I was about to hear. In my head, I pleaded and prayed, *Please, no*.

'Sexual abuse, Abdul? Why do you ask?' I said as calmly as I could.

He began to tell me the story.

There were always queues in the detention centre: boring, bleak and mindless queues, sometimes for hours and for nearly everything. There was waiting in queues for medications, for mail; sitting in the hot sun for guards to take them to school or to the hospital. There were queues every day and each time the guards would check their ID cards to examine photos and boat numbers. A person's name was on the ID card, but you would have to get close to read it; the boat number was much bigger.

To leave the detention centre for school, kids had to travel in white minibuses. It was never a matter, however, of simply hopping in and driving off, or jumping out without being checked at the other end. One day, for whatever reason, Abdul was grumpy and tired and stayed sprawled on his seat in the minibus. A female guard snapped at him to present his ID card so she could check off his boat number. Abdul refused, explaining that she knew who he was and he was sick of doing this every time. When she insisted on seeing the ID card, he snapped back, 'It's in my pocket. Take it yourself.'

A year of waiting, lining up and boat numbers had taken its toll. The guard, rather than see the situation for what it was—a depressed sixteen-year-old boy rebelling—decided that her authority was under attack and summoned another guard. With the additional pressure, Abdul changed his mind and took the card out of his pocket.

'I shouldn't have done that,' he told me. 'It wasn't good. She was just doing her job. I shouldn't have let my bad mood stop her doing her job. But then the other officer came and she told me that if I'd said that anywhere else in Australia it would be called sexual abuse.'

'How?' I asked, incredulous. 'How could a teenage boy, cornered in a seat and with witnesses all around, sexually abuse two adult guards?' If the guards chose to put their hands in his trouser pocket, wasn't that their stupid choice?

Abdul had carried deep shame and fear from this single accusation. It had affected him worse than being under the total physical control of these guards because in his inno-cence he thought he had done something terrible. As well as being labelled by the system as 'illegal', he had thought he was also seen as a 'pervert'.

One year later, this was the first time Abdul had felt safe enough to ask.

Chapter 39

PARENTING AGAINST THE ODDS

It was a normal day. The boys had all left for school, Rob had left for the hospital and I was washing the breakfast dishes before leaving for work when my phone rang, showing my middle son, Lucas's, mobile number. I answered and a woman I didn't know asked me if I was Lucas's mother . . . Then the phone shut off. Probably because I fumbled it with wet, confused hands. In the few seconds before it rang again, my anxiety levels had risen to catastrophic levels.

'Lucas has been hit by a car,' she said when we were connected again.

For that instant there was nothingness—a non-existence— then my chest folded in on itself and a black dizziness made me grab on to the bench. He had ridden his bike to school that morning and now I thought he was dead. Then outside of myself I heard the woman say that he was alive and that he was talking. I remember worrying about appearing rude when I asked if she had called an ambulance.

'You must call an ambulance. Call an ambulance now!' I said before she could even answer.

The woman, another school mum, reassured me that an ambulance had been called and that she would stay with Lucas until it arrived. I had no idea about his injuries. Had his head been hit? Was he making sense when he was talking? Had he broken any bones? Were there possible internal injuries? Or was she just keeping quiet until I could get to the scene and they could break the worst to me?

I don't know why I thought she'd know, when the ambulance hadn't even arrived, but I asked her, 'Where will they take him? What hospital?'

She didn't know.

We hung up and I rang Rob, who had a patient under anaesthetic in the middle of surgery. I didn't want to put him through what I just had experienced, but when I tried to speak the words wouldn't come out.

'Lucas . . .' I sobbed.

'What?'

I couldn't speak.

'*What is it?*' he asked more urgently.

'He's been . . . hit by a car . . . I think he's okay. I'm going to see him.'

My husband is a good person to have around in a bad situation, and he seemed to keep it together on the phone.

'Okay,' he said. 'I'm going to finish up here. Tell me where he is and I'll meet you there.'

When I arrived at the school an ambulance was parked on the other side of the road. I raced across the street to find Lucas sitting inside, quiet and pale. I was not reassured and asked the paramedics if he'd been knocked out.

'No.'

'Did people see?'

'Yes, there were witnesses,' the paramedic replied.

'Are you sore anywhere else?' I asked Lucas anxiously. 'Are you sure? Have you checked?'

He wiggled his arms and legs and patted his head. Finally, I accepted that apart from some nasty-looking abrasions and maybe a sprained ankle Lucas was okay.

I was aware that the driver of the huge four-wheel drive was waiting in the background, but I could not think about him. Later, I was told that while he was still sprawled on the road, my dear, gentle son apologised to the driver.

On the way home, we said little to each other than 'I love you' because we were both in shock. Lucas, because he knew how close he came to losing his life, and me, because this morning when I did not know if Lucas had died my whole world had disappeared. Once inside the shelter of home, we sat on the lounge and I held him close until I could feel he was getting restless. Then I washed his abrasions and covered him with blankets.

Later that day, a tidal wave of emotion crashed in on me. A million thoughts went through my mind and yet I couldn't think: fragments of pain interspersed with emptiness. When

Abdul came home, he wiped the tears from my cheeks and eyes with both his thumbs before putting his arm around me.

'It's okay,' he murmured. 'He's okay.'

When Rob came home later that evening, having earlier been reassured that everything was fine, we held each other, not speaking.

Over the next week, I had trouble getting to sleep and frequently woke with jolts of dread. I had nightmares about all sorts of catastrophes and tears came out of the blue.

My mind turned to Zaynab and all she had been through. I wondered how parents like her manage in situations of war and trauma that affect every aspect of life every single day. How do you continue to live if the worst does happen, as it did for Zaynab? I thought about her waking up in a hospital bed to hear that her little boy, Abdul and Ahad's oldest brother, had been blown apart by the Taliban rocket that had targeted their house. I had only just learned this. The boys said that Zaynab didn't even have even one photograph to remember her dead son by. Just that thought alone broke my heart . . . Imagine not having even one photo of your beloved stolen child?

Ahad, who was just a baby at the time, didn't remember anything of the attack except that, according to his mother, he is very lucky to be alive. The boys later told me how, when their mother cuddled them, they could feel the lumps of shrapnel that remained in her shoulder. What memories, I wonder, are triggered for Zaynab each time she touches her own shoulder? I know she is a strong woman, but no one is unscathed after losing a child. How does she live with that loss, and with the ongoing threats and risks to her family every day?

When Ahad and Abdul were children, there were many occasions when Zaynab's strength did break down. Abdul once told me he had coaxed her to smile and to eat again by chewing on eggshells, saying, 'Look, even these are yummy!' In Australia, whenever Abdul and Ahad insisted that it was my bed time or that I needed to eat, I became irritated, wrongly attributing this to a controlling, gender-based 'cultural' quirk, but now I recognise this solicitousness is more likely a linger-ing shadow of care for a traumatised mother who had her world ripped apart. The trouble with this early independence for children, and especially if they take on a role of looking after adults, is that they learn to minimise their own emo-tional needs. This can make it hard for the child to ask for help when they need it themselves, which in turn makes them vulnerable: we humans need each other in times of stress.

The violence of war touches more than just families. It affects food supplies and nutrition, it blocks access to medical care, and it can destroy community structures and supports, including education and public order. War and ongoing safety concerns constrict people's lives.

As children grow older, their world needs to expand, but what if that world is already unsafe? What if sending a child out to school, or to buy food, or to help run a business, or to attend mosque has dangers? Any of these places are system-atically targeted by terrorists in Afghanistan. Parents living in places of instability face the dilemma of either striving to live a normal life for their children or submitting to the terrorists' agenda and leaving their children hungry, uneducated and isolated from community and culture.

Parents' emotional trauma also has an intergenerational impact. Multiple generations in Afghanistan have seen people being killed and have likely been under attack themselves. They have lost loved ones to violence or have experienced their parents' and carers' emotional disconnection due to resultant mental illness. As decades of medical research has established, childhood trauma has enduring effects on health and on the brain's hormonal and behavioural reactions to future stress.

So how can parents protect their children in situations of war and trauma that affect every single aspect of every single day? Such stress is too big for anyone to cope with. The trouble is that parenting is a full-time job; there is no break. What happens when parents lose their reserves and the capacity to help their children manage trauma?

For families who have fled from traumatic situations and arrived in Australia by boat, the stress does not stop here. Detention deprives children of confident parenting. In detention, I witnessed parents unable to make decisions about even basic health care for their children or the food they receive, while sleeping children were routinely woken through the night for head counts. In the detention centres, I have heard parents expressing their hopelessness and suicidality in front of their children, and I have seen parents who could not look their children in the eye because they were so ashamed of the decisions that had landed them in such a situation. My colleagues have told me of parents who had lost all capacity to manage themselves, let alone their babies. I have also witnessed adults who, because of their own mental health issues, were unable to see their child's needs. Sadly, as a psychiatrist, I know the evidence unequivocally shows that Australia's treatment of asylum seekers, especially children, causes longstanding harm to their mental health and development. Yet, these harmful government policies persist despite warnings from all of Australia's peak medical bodies.

Once parents and their children are out of detention their problems don't let up. Asylum seekers on temporary visas are still denied hope and security, social security payments needed for food and day-to-day survival are cut, and even medical services are denied. They live every day with the threat of being returned hanging over their heads. In situations like these, how does one build a life and recover?

xxxxxxx

I once took Abdul to the Australian War Memorial. I was worried that this might be too much for him, but he was insistent. As we viewed some sandbag barriers in the World War I exhibit, he told me that, as a child, he used to play in places like these. He pointed out the Russian AK-47 assault rifles, PK machine guns and the US-made M16 rifles, all of which were familiar to him. Even the bolt-action rifles from a century ago were still in Afghanistan. He nodded in recognition at a white UN Land Rover, but when we entered a room with the booming overhead sounds of planes and explosions we both flinched. Abdul was delighted to see a battered black Phoenix bike in a room dedicated to

Afghanistan because it was just like one his family had. I did not point out that this particular bike had been part of a nasty IED (improvised explosive device) in Kabul.

xxxxxxx

My eldest son, Jasper, likes making stuff. He has made a smelter to melt down and mould old aluminium cans into paperweights, and he has developed security systems for his bedroom and a robot that can plant seeds. When he was in Year Nine, he made a gun out of PVC pipe that I immediately confiscated when he showed me how it could shoot a marble straight through a tin of tomatoes. Unfortunately, I did not discover a later, much larger version that launched tennis balls across the valley until I came across Jasper showing it to the Afghan boys. Ahad had already assumed the one-kneed crouching position of infantry, with this mortar supported over his shoulder.

When we have played games like hide-and-seek, Abdul always wins because he just melts away and can't be found. Once I cheated and looked to see how he did it. His entire demeanour became serious as he dropped low to the ground, perfectly silent with every nerve twitching and every sense alert. I realised, then, that Abdul can never just play at this. For him, this game was survival.

In Afghanistan, Abdul and Ahad had to leave the house and face risk each day in order to help the family. That they were also specifically targeted and threatened was among the reasons they had to leave Afghanistan. These boys have faced more danger than we can imagine and have seen things that the word 'horrible' can't even begin to describe. It makes my insistence on them wearing a bike helmet or worrying about Abdul going to boxing training seem petty.

That parents endure almost unimaginable hardship and continue to live is a testament to the resilience of the human spirit. Thinking about what other parents have had to face makes me hold my children a little closer at night, thankful that some of us have been lucky enough to be born in Australia.

Chapter 40

REMEMBERING

What would it be like, as a child, to witness the worst that humans can inflict on each other? It is one thing to diagnose and treat PTSD from a safe emotional distance as a psychiatrist, but quite another to see loved ones suffering the torments and paralysis of PTSD and depression.

Trauma is a poison. No matter how brave or resilient a person is, if they have a large enough dose of psychological trauma they can develop PTSD, and the more accumulated trauma a person experiences, the more likely it is they will succumb to it.

One of my patients once described traumatic memories as 'digging up graves', but memories are only part of the problem in PTSD. There are also painful emotions such as fear, sadness, shame and anger that are difficult to control.

Sometimes all emotion is numbed and it can be hard to even think. In severe trauma, not only is there often conscious avoidance of the memories, the body and brain can also take over to protect the person's daily life by making it hard, or even impossible, to remember details of the event. The disorder affects the body's responses and one's internal sense of being.

The experience of being completely at the mercy of a traumatic event that makes a person feel they are being treated as less than human can shatter one's sense of self and existence. Witnessing horror can also erode trust: for many, no part of the world is safe anymore. Treatment can help, but once broken these things can never be rebuilt to what they were.

Rob tells me that when he anaesthetises someone with PTSD, he can tell trauma is not just present in the brain but also lives in the body.

'When I see them in prep, they're obviously tense. When I get them to sleep and they're deep down, they still don't tone down well. Their heart rate and blood pressure are up and you can see it in their skin. They are even wound up under a general anaesthetic.'

I don't know all that Abdul and Ahad have been through. Most people with PTSD don't like to talk about the incidents that have caused it and it's not helpful for me to potentially re-traumatise them by asking about things they would prefer to forget. But I do know the experience of detention was traumatic for them.

'You know I have been through a lot in my life, and have had some tough and horrible experiences,' Abdul once said to me. 'But being in detention was one of the toughest and most horrible experiences of my life.'

When Abdul first came to live with us he needed to visit the GP. Waiting in the surgery reception, fenced all around by skinny-legged plastic chairs and a wall feature of grey rocks, Abdul seemed to disappear. He stopped talking, his eyes glazed over, his body constricted and he began to shiver uncontrollably. All I could do was wrap my arms around his shoulders and rock him gently, like I would a baby, until he gradually came out of it. Later, Abdul told me that the waiting room reminded him of being back in Darwin, trapped and alone.

One night, I asked him to take me on an internet exploration of Afghanistan to find his village in the region of Hazarajat. On the computer screen, we zoomed in to grey, sharp-pointed mountains and valleys lined with watercourses more lush and green than I had expected. Abdul found one of the only roads from Kabul to Hazarajat and showed me where it wound through a beautiful valley famous for growing apples. It is also a valley where the Taliban ambush travellers, usually Hazaras. They torture their victims before executing them and mutilating their bodies, sometimes taking videos to be later found by the grieving relatives.

I could see Abdul was rattled by what he just told me, so I suggested we visit Kabul instead. He showed me some of the important buildings. How beautiful they must have been before they were destroyed by bombs or pockmarked with shrapnel. Abdul showed me the district in Kabul he had lived in after fleeing Hazarajat and the mountains he explored with his friends. He showed me another mountain near Kabul that had a big wall running across it and explained that it had been built by enslaved Hazaras centuries ago.

For the rest of the tour, Abdul pointed out where various explosions had happened; the expected pattern of terrorist attacks is two bombs, he said. The second bomb targets the people coming in to help those injured by the first. He told me about a bomb that had exploded near the river and how people had jumped into the water to escape—only to drown instead. He showed me the place where he had narrowly escaped being blown apart in the Afghan winter of 2011. He didn't offer any further information about what had happened to him that day and I didn't ask, but I've seen him flinch at loud noises, at explosions on television, or the depiction of pumping blood.

The attack that nearly claimed Abdul's life occurred on the Holy Day of Ashura, the day Shia Muslims commemorate the martyr death of Hussein, Muhammad's grandson, in 680 AD. A suicide bomber had been lying in wait at the Abu Fazal shrine at midday in order to maximise the number of victims—over 50 people died that day; many were babies. *The New York Times* published a photograph of a girl aged about eleven or twelve standing frozen in a scream. Her green dress, scarf and white leggings were covered in blood, while heaped around her were the lifeless bodies of other children. Injured adults, bloodied and dazed, were sitting around, staring. Back in 2011, this news had passed me by. Now, hearing that Abdul had been there, this mere newspaper article is terrifying enough to make my stomach and chest contract and give me nightmares.

Mostly the day-to-day realities of bombings and murders and kidnappings in Afghanistan did not reach the Australian news, but when a particularly bad event happened, or there was a suggestion that Abdul and Ahad's family were threatened, the boys became preoccupied and unsettled for weeks. I once told Abdul that I wished I could take all of his bad memories and nightmares, double plastic bag them, and lock them in the deep freeze.

'But you can't. My memories are me, this is who I am,' he responded. He had been clutching at a biro and unknowingly scratched a deep groove into our already battered kitchen table.

Sleep is also a big problem for those who suffer PTSD. For the first year he lived with us, Abdul did not get to sleep most nights until 2 a.m., sometimes later. When Ahad moved in, the boys slept together, as they had all their lives in Afghanistan. This seemed to help, but once on a trip to Sydney I woke with a start at about 3 a.m. Abdul was sitting bolt upright in the bed he was sharing with Ahad, crying, moaning and pleading in Hazaragi. In the darkness, I watched Ahad quietly soothe his brother back to sleep.

PTSD can make people unable to tolerate any intense emotions, and conflict with others can be difficult too. At times, when his emotions became disorganised, Abdul was convinced no one cared and he simply couldn't remember any of the good things we had together. And when Abdul and I had our 'lively discussions', which were not even arguments, or when the younger boys were squabbling with each other at home, Ahad became distressed.

PTSD can cause people to become out of synch in their interactions with others. When one's world view has been destroyed, it is often hard to understand those who have not been traumatised. The brain pathways affected by the PTSD means it can be difficult to try new things. Emotions are either detached or people fear their emotions will become too overwhelming for others—these things lead to estrangement and isolation, and a feeling of being stuck.

Back when he lived with us, Ahad would come along to a family event or excursion, but often he wasn't really *there*. A veil came between us. During these times, his body and mind were struggling to deal with the noise and intensity of our family and he could only cope by disconnecting. I know this is not how he has always been. Abdul once described another Ahad, the child he was back in Afghanistan.

'Loud, like if he swallowed a speaker. Fast like a bullet. Very cheeky, talkative and very funny. Sometimes he was so annoying that I wanted to tell him shut up, but he was too funny and I couldn't stop laughing. Everyone loved him because he was warm and cute. He was so creative with the way he was making jokes. Some used to call him *khosh*, which means happy. Some also used to call him *qerti*, which is a word for someone who jumps around and has lots of energy. He couldn't even sit somewhere for a minute!'

When I saw glimpses of this happier Ahad, I knew he was still there. But now it seemed as if he preferred to be left alone. I wish I had met Ahad earlier, and I also wish that the people and service providers who could have looked after him as a teenager in Brisbane had done more.

I can't be Abdul's and Ahad's therapist. I can't listen to all the boys' stories. It is too hard for me because of my attachment to them. Their stories affect me too much emotionally and physically. But I can support Abdul and Ahad by helping them feel they matter and that they have a purpose in life. I can encourage them to stay healthy by avoiding alcohol and drugs as a means of escaping their pain. I can also encourage them to exercise because exercise helps our bodies (and emotions) stay regulated. And I will always try to be there for them. My greatest fear, though, is that the boys will not ask for help when the darkness and horrors become too much.

Chapter 41

VISAS

Abdul arrived on Christmas Island on 8 August 2013 and remained in detention until 22 December 2014, a period of 500 days. Then, after almost a year of living with us, under community detention, the Department of Immigration finally invited him to put his case forward as a refugee. The government referred to that process as lifting the 'bar' (which refers to their decision to stop looking at any appeals for refugee status for around 30,000 people and which had prevented him from putting his case as a refugee across when he first arrived on our shores). The interview was set for the end of 2015 on the day that happened to be Abdul's eighteenth birthday. As the name implies, under the Fast-Track assessment, shortcuts are taken in the refugee assessment process—hazardous shortcuts that are neither safe nor fair for refugees. We were about to see it in action.

Only one interview is conducted, during which time the applicant must supply documentation to prove he or she is a genuine refugee. No new information will be accepted after this single interview, despite it being well recognised that traumatised people can have hazy memories around these events. Under the old legislation, the department's decisions could be re-evaluated formally by the Refugee Review Tribunal, but this safeguard no longer exists. Now, if a review of the department's decision to refuse refugee status is requested, all that can happen is that the original paperwork will be re-read. A person whose genuine concerns have been missed faces the life-threatening situation of being deported. An additional interview is not allowed, and there is no recourse to any independent organisation for appeals. This whole assessment process is now outside the safeguards of the UN Refugee Convention.

In reality, the swift processing of refugee claims the government touted has not eventuated. After several years, thousands of people remain unprocessed, while the rate of rejections is significantly higher than under the former process that had more checks and balances. Rejections can't be appealed. The new system also means that even if the applicant is found to be a genuine refugee, the most he or she can expect is a three-year Temporary Protection Visa (TPV), or a five-year Safe Haven Enterprise Visa (SHEV), at the end of which the administrative process, and the anguish for a person fearful of being returned, starts all over again.

A TPV entitles the refugee to three years in Australia.

They can work and access Medicare and Centrelink in some circumstances, but they are not able to undertake tertiary studies. The SHEV is for five years, but for three and a half years of it the person must work or study full-time in a designated regional area and not be on social benefits. If applying for tertiary studies, they will not get any government allowances in most cases and must also pay the higher international student fees upfront. SHEV holders may be able to apply for another type of visa later, such as a work, study or family visa, but there is no sign of the government being agreeable to any sort of permanency. Because education is so important to Abdul and he wanted the chance to go to university, he thought he would apply for a SHEV.

Both TPV and SHEV holders must obtain approval from the minister to travel overseas for 'compassionate or compelling circumstances' but they cannot travel to the country from which they sought protection. Neither the TPV nor the SHEV will allow the holder to sponsor family members to come to Australia. The application itself is very complex, over 40 pages long with over 100 questions. The form is only available in English, another barrier. And, at the same time, most asylum seekers' access to federally funded legal aid and translation services has been stopped.

Knowing how much rode on this process, I tried to do as much baseline preparation as possible: once Abdul was invited to submit his application, the timeframe to make his case before the interview would be extremely tight. This included helping Abdul request his immigration department file through the Freedom of Information Act. We needed to know that all the information immigration had gathered on him was correct.

One evening I arrived home to an atmosphere of tense unhappiness. While making dinner, I found a letter addressed to Abdul from the Department of Immigration in the kitchen bin. The letter informed him that it was refusing his Freedom of Information request because Immigration and Border Protection had not yet 'invited' Abdul to an interview. It then told him, in a scolding tone, to 'wait his turn' to get his paperwork. Hanging over Abdul's head was the constant worry that he could be sent back to Afghanistan, or to permanent detention. This fear sapped him of the energy needed for the arduous process of preparing and he was often close to giving up. He had screwed the letter up and thrown it away in despair.

I was furious. Apart from some isolated national security cases, everyone, including non-citizens, has the right to access information held on them by Australian public authorities. This right is not affected by an agency or by the minister's belief as to why a person could want these documents. In this instance, the department had trampled on the Freedom of Information Act. Its refusal had also contravened the Australian cultural imperative of 'a fair go'.

After giving Abdul a lecture on his rights, about not giving up, and about the fine Australian tradition of 'keeping the bastards honest', we requested a review of this decision, reminding the department of their obligations under the law. Soon after, the 1211 pages of documentation from immigration, and its contracted health company, IHMS, arrived.

Chapter 42

THE 'FAST-TRACK' INTERVIEW

Abdul, unhappy to see his file because it was a reminder of his time in detention, went into a decline. He did, however, allow me to read through the paperwork alone. It was gruelling to have my dear Abdul continually referred to merely as his boat number, HYN071, or as a UAM (unaccompanied minor), rather than by his name.

When he first received the letter to say the department wanted to review his asylum status, Abdul was still seventeen. Since he had arrived as an unaccompanied child, he was able to access assistance through the Refugee Advice and Casework Service (RACS). RACS is a community legal centre in Sydney that provides asylum seekers and refugees with free legal advice and assistance. Abdul's lawyer, who prefers to stay anonymous so I will give her the pseudonym of 'Verity', meaning truth, was awesome—it's an overused word but entirely appropriate in her case. People like her do not do their job for the money or for the accolades. Every working day, and likely at great emotional cost, she hears horrific stories and then turns them into a concise legal document for the most basic of reasons: justice.

In order to prove Abdul's claim for refugee status, he needed to recount his life story to Verity so she could produce a document for immigration. This was not an easy task for any of us. She and I were driven to distraction because Abdul did not want to talk about the horrible things that had happened to him. We had to plead for him to tell his story, reminding him that it was absolutely necessary to give a picture of why he had fled Afghanistan and why he was still at risk. This was not unusual: as a psychiatrist, I have seen police officers and soldiers with PTSD almost sacrifice their pensions to avoid the distress of having to recount their story to bureaucrats.

Compelling people with PTSD to relive their memories is risky. It can drive people into a crisis, and trained professionals are careful about how they can help a patient divulge details of their trauma. Verity spent many hours with Abdul and an interpreter, and eventually his story came out. Then, over many weeks, she helped him write his application.

The ordeal of preparing his case was nearly too much for Abdul. So often throughout this process he would say to us, 'I don't need to beg, they know what is happening in Afghanistan. If they don't believe me or don't want me, they can take me to Nauru, they can send me to Afghanistan. I don't care.' In those weeks and months before his interview, Abdul disappeared into himself. The light in his bedroom window was often on well into the early morning and each day he left for school drained and weighed down. It was hard to give Abdul hope when his underlying belief, based on experience, was that the whole exercise was futile. 'They can do whatever they want to me whenever they feel like it,' he would say.

Abdul tried to make himself happy whenever he could— so much so it was hard to witness. Many days were spent in a frenzy of distracting activity: trips away, seeing all he could, and feeling he had to live and breathe this life in Australia in case he was taken away. I colluded with him in his efforts. I wanted to fill him with good memories should the worst happen.

I had made an arty notice for the wall at this time, partly for Abdul and also for my boys, who, when they reached thirteen or so started to be less affectionate and frankly awkward if I offered them a cuddle. The sign read 'Everyone needs a daily hug' and its purpose was for them to not feel so self-conscious about getting a hug from me. I noticed that Abdul pointed to the sign and collected his hug each day and it seemed to work for the other boys too, which was reassuring. These hugs, trips and fun activities were entertaining for all the boys, but there was not much time left over for Rob and me. I wondered if I should make an arty notice for us and what I would put on it.

xxxxxxx

Verity took time describing the process that would take place at the Sydney immigration office. The interview would likely take four or five hours. Present would be staff from immigration, an interpreter, an independent observer and herself. She stressed that the immigration examiners would spend a lot of time on establishing Abdul's identity and obtaining identity documents. They would also ask detailed questions about his family and what had happened to them. Abdul would also have to describe the times he and his family had been directly at risk and why he feared harm if returned to Afghanistan.

'Why couldn't you live somewhere else in Afghanistan and why couldn't the authorities protect you? Why, after all this time, are you still unsafe? Why can't you return to Afghanistan?'

They would ask the same questions in different ways because they were trying to trip him up, Verity said. She prepared him for an interrogation. She encouraged Abdul to take his time and, despite the close questioning, not to become flustered or frustrated. She knew that recounting his traumatic history to this audience would be a gruelling and distressing process and reminded him that he could ask for breaks. The stakes were too high to make errors or for him to try to push through just to get it done with as quickly as possible. Even though there would be pressure from the interviewer, Abdul needed to take his time to answer the questions the way he needed to.

Verity stressed that he always had to be truthful and if he didn't remember or didn't know something then he needed to say so. She also strongly encouraged him to use the interpreter if there were any doubts about what was being asked or if he was confused. Finally, Verity emphasised that Abdul needed to tell immigration everything he could remember, because after this one interview immigration would accept no further evidence to support his claim for refugee status.

xxxxxxx

Rather than driving an anxious four hours the morning of the interview, Abdul and I stayed in Parramatta the night before. Parramatta is a thriving multicultural municipality of Sydney, and a good psychological distance away from the immigration offices near Central Station. That night, as we sat at the street table of a Thai restaurant along busy Church Street, we almost had fun. Abdul hadn't eaten Thai food before and thought it was delicious. He pointed out a Hazara family walking by and told me that the husband was being severely told off by his wife. Then an Iraqi family walked past and he translated a little of what he could understand of their conversation. Sitting with this young polyglot was like having a front row seat to life! Abdul needled me about the two cocktails I had with dinner. I didn't tell him that I was worrying about the next day and hoped they would help me sleep.

The next morning, I bought Abdul a 'happy eighteenth birthday' coffee before we took the train into the city for the midday appointment. It didn't feel like a birthday celebration should and our mood was subdued. I feared that today would be the last one he had free.

As we approached the immigration building, we saw Karim, Abdul's friend from Canberra. He was also Hazara and had just finished his interview. They shook hands and each boy put his right hand over his heart. That Karim had not been dragged away by Border Force officers gave me some relief. Their quiet chat together was also a reassuring island of normality in this oppressive day.

Abdul and I took the elevator to the appointed floor in silence. There were several people already in the waiting room, but no one was talking. To distract ourselves, we exchanged silly faces. In time, Verity arrived and made a few encouraging remarks before disappearing into an office. Abdul's independent observer arrived to introduce himself and soon left, and some minutes later the immigration officer asked Abdul to accompany her into the interview room. I gave Abdul a hug and reminded him to try his hardest to tell all of his story. In my heart, I said goodbye.

While I waited, I had plenty of time to look around. There were a series of plaques on the wall noting the department's name changes. It was first called the Department of Immigration and Multiculturalism, reliving a time of welcome and celebration of diversity. Then it became the utilitarian Department of Immigration and Citizenship before paranoia set in with the Department of Immigration and Border Protection.

I recoiled at the dismissive way the frontline office staff spoke to each client, and it was disconcerting to hear them discussing other applicants' personal circumstances in my hearing. When I let the security guard sitting in his little cubicle know there was no toilet paper in the bathrooms, he told me there was no point replacing it. 'They steal it,' he said in a contemptuous tone.

Five hours later, Abdul came out of the interview room pale and shrunken. Verity, by contrast, was still impeccably groomed and unruffled. She commended him for telling his

story, but explained that there were some technical legal difficulties with Abdul's submission, namely that he didn't have
his Taskera (Afghan ID card) and immigration insisted on
him getting the original despite it being impossible. Another
hiccup was that Ahad, unbeknownst to any of us, had in fact
applied for a humanitarian visa for Abdul several years ago.
Apparently, this visa application had sat in a drawer in immigration all this time, unprocessed, and now it could be used
against Abdul. If immigration chose to be parsimonious, they
could refuse to process the new visa Abdul was applying for
and all the pain and effort would have been for nothing.

Abdul was dazed. We walked away from the office with
these new uncertainties and fears and sat for several hours
on the lawns outside Central Station in silence. So much for
'Fast-Track'. Little did we know that it would take another
424 days for the department to give Abdul an answer as to
what they would allow his future to be.

xxxxxxx

For weeks Abdul was in despair, and his youth worker, who I
hoped would make contact to support him, remained absent.
But there was already a history of this lack of engagement
and of me calling them in exasperation. One youth worker had
dropped seventeen-year-old Abdul off in a deserted school-
yard at 11 p.m. to find his own way home after an event and
nearly every time a youth worker was supposed to process the
paperwork required for Abdul to go away on holidays with us
they missed the deadline.

The non-government organisation that employs these

youth workers is not a benevolent charity to be let off the hook because underneath it has 'good intentions'. The company is paid handsomely by the Department of Immigration, and its employees are paid to do a professional job. Every time they fail there are ramifications for those who rely on them. So many times it has appeared to me that rather than being advocates for their vulnerable charges, they have instead been lackeys for the Department of Immigration.

Then one day Abdul was summoned to a new youth worker's place of work. It had previously been a group home for young asylum seekers and was mostly empty during the day. It was important that they talk in person, the youth worker insisted, but she refused tell Abdul or myself why.

In order to help build on this relationship, I suggested *she* join *us* for a cup of tea in Abdul's home and we could have the discussion there. I thought this could also give her the chance to inspect his living conditions, which I naively imagined was part of her job. Another reason for the invitation was the fear that the Border Force heavies could be waiting at the group home to take him away.

She refused our invitation and insisted that Abdul come to her, citing safety concerns about her breaking boundaries if she met with a teenage boy in his own home with carers present. I say carer, but to immigration and the case worker I had no role whatsoever except as a detention custodian. She preferred, too, that he come by himself. Abdul was not keen on this idea and neither was I. In the end, I came to the interview to provide support—and to drive around the neighbourhood in advance to make sure Border Force was not there.

It turned out that the matter to be discussed was a bridging visa while his refugee application was being assessed. The bridging visa was another form of temporary status given while the TPV or SHEV was being determined. A bridging visa meant Abdul was no longer in community detention, so he wouldn't have a curfew anymore, but there were other rules and a code of conduct that needed to be read out to him via teleconference with immigration. Then he had to sign the agreement in front of his youth worker. This activity made it very clear that these employees were, in reality, doing the job of immigration in Sydney who needed to outsource their duties. During the teleconference, the immigration officer on the other end of the line mentioned several times that Abdul was 'illegal'.

Once the conference call was finished, I reminded Abdul and his youth worker that he was not illegal. His youth worker shook her head in disagreement, so I laboured the point: to be called illegal was not only incorrect, but it was extremely distressing to asylum seekers, the very people she was supposed to be caring for. This woman, whose ignorance was appalling, and who was supposed to be looking after Abdul's social and emotional wellbeing, argued back, replying that of course Abdul was illegal, that's why he was in detention. The irony that she had come to Australia as an immigrant herself yet was so unwelcoming was apparently lost on her, but not on us. As we walked away, I knew more damage had been done.

After the meeting, I emailed the organisation suggesting that perhaps those with some responsibility for these children's welfare should not perpetuate the distress with their ignorance. Yet again, there was no reply.

Chapter 43

SHOULDER SURGERY

Abdul had been riding a bicycle in Kabul when he was hit by a car. The driver sped off. With his shoulder forced out of its socket, Abdul had no choice but to hold on to a pole on the side of the road and pull the joint back in himself, after which he fainted from the pain. After this accident, his shoulder was so damaged and weak that it would dislocate on a regular basis—probably over 40 times to date. Sometimes it would just slip out of place or dislocate from his thrashing during a nightmare, and each time it caused severe pain and immobility. In fact, Abdul was in pain far more often than he let on, but because the medications made him drowsy and complacent, he preferred to bear the discomfort instead.

When his shoulder popped out on Christmas Island the first time, the nurse on duty assumed he was malingering and refused to call the doctor. For the next eighteen hours, all he was given was an icepack and a few Panadol. Before I studied psychiatry, I worked as an emergency registrar, and I know that dislocated shoulders can cause such spasms and agony that they usually require muscle relaxants and opioid analgesics, such as morphine. They also need immediate treatment. The longer the dislocation is left untreated, the more the muscles around the shoulder go into spasm, which increases the pain and makes it harder to put back. Abdul's stoic nature and high pain threshold did him no favours.

Abdul told me that the Serco guards looking after him became distressed about his lack of medical attention because they could see he was in agony. One of them was so appalled that he suggested to Abdul that a lawyer should have been involved.

Intriguingly, all medical file notes about that particular night were missing from the medical file that we later obtained under the FOI Act. I hope these missing notes were due to shoddy performance by the file team of the Department of Immigration since the alternative—that medical notes were deliberately tampered with—would be egregious behaviour. All that is left is a doctor's letter stating that Abdul's arm was hard to put back because of the delay in consultation.

Eventually he did have treatment, requiring heavy sedation. He had several further dislocations on Christmas Island, followed by weeks of pain spent with his right arm in a sling. He was told that he couldn't go to school if he couldn't write, so over a single weekend Abdul taught himself to write, in English, with his left hand.

His shoulder, which was becoming progressively more damaged and urgently needed surgery, was the only reason Abdul was transferred to Darwin from Christmas Island rather than being sent to Nauru. The wait list for surgery in Darwin, however, was long. Now perhaps we should be thankful for that: if his shoulder had been fixed earlier, he would have been sent to Nauru and he would not be with us now.

Once Abdul moved to Canberra the whole process of assessing his shoulder had to start all over again, including seeing a GP, waiting for an initial assessment through the orthopaedic clinic at the Canberra Hospital, and then being put on the waiting list for a public MRI. Although we offered to pay for his treatment ourselves to hurry the process along, IHMS would not allow it.

The thought of surgery terrified Abdul. As far as he was concerned, going into hospital meant a reasonable probability of never coming out again. Rob and I spent a lot of time reassuring him about the skill of his surgeon and anaesthetist, talked him through the steps of his hospital stay and procedure, and urged him to tell the nurses if he was in pain. We also told him that in Australian hospitals he would be listened to. We also finally persuaded him to tell Zaynab about his surgery. He had wanted to protect her from worrying and so had not breathed a word about any of his ordeal.

When the operation finally happened, it was a few days before Christmas, some weeks after his Fast-Track interview, and almost a year after he moved in with us. By then Abdul was prepared. Because the damage was more severe than the surgeon had anticipated, the operation took longer than expected. I waited for him in his hospital room and he was eventually wheeled in, asleep on the trolley. Later, as he roused in a daze, Abdul looked around in confusion and distress until his eyes caught mine. I saw him smile in recognition and relief before he drifted back to sleep. For me, this moment made it all worthwhile.

To watch what Abdul achieved during his recovery, with his arm strapped to his chest, was awe-inspiring. Perhaps a better word is amusing. Abdul is a positive and determined boy, but many times I do wonder if he is a little hare-brained, too. He played left-handed tennis, rode his bike, pushed himself to go swimming and even went boogie boarding in the surf with his good arm.

Today Abdul still stands holding his right elbow. It has become a habit, but now he has freedom from pain. And, most importantly, he has the freedom to again use his body and to push himself with confidence.

Chapter 44

HE'S GETTING YOUNGER

It was a hot, bright-blue Australian summer day during the end-of-year holidays. Rob was at work on call and Jasper and Lucas were out with friends. Abdul, Toby and I spent the day at a swimming hole in the bush. The cicadas were noisy and, at times, it was hard to hear each other as we walked down the rocky track to a magical place where the Shoalhaven River expands out into a deep pool of fresh, cool water. As if by design, there is a ledge for jumping from and the gentle current makes swimming in one direction beautifully relaxing. Coming back is a different matter.

It was only ten days after Abdul's shoulder surgery. His arm was still tender and held in place by a complicated sling. When I suggested the outing, I worried that he may have been frustrated about not being able to swim, but Abdul assured me that he would enjoy coming, even if it meant sitting by the side of the river.

Toby raced to the water's edge and was off—splashing and yelling at us to jump in, too. Picking my way over the jumble of rocks, I gradually lowered myself into the cool water. Toby, by this time, had disappeared with the current around the corner. Suddenly Abdul dived into the water with his right arm tied against his body and shot past me. Of course he wouldn't let a simple thing like major shoulder surgery stop him!

Feeling the weight of responsibility, I raced after them, working hard to keep both in sight as we were swept along by the current, flying past the reeds on one side and the rocky wall on the other. Swimming with just one arm, Abdul had caught up to Toby and, with a whoop, dived under the water, resurfacing past him. Abdul and Toby dived down again and when they bobbed up, with hair shiny and dark and slicked down, they looked like brother seals.

Seeing that Abdul could only sidestroke, I tried out his technique only to discover how hard it was. My initial concern for Abdul's safety turned into strong pride for his determination and stamina. After a few hours, we swam back upstream to our picnic spot on the hot sand of the riverbank and had lunch. Later in the afternoon, as I sat in the shade watching the boys catch tiny fish with their bare hands, I realised Abdul had become younger.

The photo on Abdul's detention ID card was taken soon after he'd been plucked off the boat, badly sunburned, having had no sleep and little food and water for three days. In the photo, he looked as though he could have been a 24 year old.

When I first got to know him, despite his lovely smiles, Abdul held himself in a solemn, almost grave, manner, similar to the way I have observed other Hazara men behave. This may have been politeness, but looking more closely I also knew that some parts inside of him had shut down. Stress had aged this boy, and with each visit to the detention centre I saw he was getting worse.

Since Abdul moved in with us, I'd become exasperated at times when I thought he wasn't acting his age, which was unfair, especially as I had previously told Abdul that I was looking forward to him becoming a little cheeky and challenging. His silly behaviour showed me that he felt safe enough to test the limits, as teenagers ought to do.

Abdul had grown taller, and his face had changed its boyish profile from when I first met him. But despite these maturing changes, Abdul still looks younger than he did back then. The shut-down and haunted look has mostly gone and his face is more relaxed, open and reactive. As I watched him that day, playing in the water with his brother, I was happy that Abdul had not yet forgotten how to be a child.

Chapter 45

THE ASSAULT

In the first few weeks after Abdul's Fast-Track interview, we were on tenterhooks, not daring to push immigration for an answer, but it appeared that 'Slow-Track' was the way it was to be. We came to the realisation that Abdul would not hear anything on his immigration case for a long time. The stress of being in community detention, his pending interview and all that it brought up for him meant that 2015 was basically written-off in terms of schooling.

He chose, in 2016, to start again. A different school, and a new start to Year Eleven. Abdul chose the school that Ahad had been to, which was much closer to our house. Most importantly, at this new school he would enter as a main-stream student because the year before, even though he was allowed to attend regular classes, he felt he was treated differently. This year was also the chance to do the outdoor education program, which sounded just like Abdul's cup of tea. The new school year started and he engaged readily with the teachers and students. He established a group of Australian friends almost immediately. That he was popular was no surprise, but only then did I realise the difference from last year, when he had not brought even one Australian school friend home.

So far 2016 was going well. Abdul was very keen to be involved in everything. There were other issues, of course. There was the incident of Abdul's hobbling out of the emergency department at 6 a.m., despite the provisional diagnosis of appendicitis, because he was so keen to go on a biology excursion to Dubbo. After waiting up with him all night in the emergency department, I was left to tell the nurses that he had nicked off, which to me was extra shameful because this was the hospital where I worked. When Abdul wasn't found back at home, I headed him off at the school where the bus was waiting, talked to his teacher and dragged him back to hospital, where we waited until the following evening. It turned out, after I been awake for 36 hours, that it wasn't appendicitis but a virus.

On an afternoon in April, a few weeks after the hospital incident, I was sitting alone in the kitchen, staring into space and nursing a cup of tea. It had been a gruelling day already with back-to-back patients in my clinic. Rob was away, and I was just about to head off again to do an evening ward round at the hospital. A depressing glance around the kitchen told me that none of the boys had bothered to clean up after their afternoon feast. It looked as if a food bomb had gone off.

The night before, Abdul and I had had another squabble and I was still feeling sensitive when he slinked in with his hoodie pulled over his head and loitered in front of the open freezer door for what seemed a long time.

'Do we have any ice blocks?' he muttered from under his hood, finally acknowledging my presence.

'Shut the bloody fridge door,' I snapped back, my annoyance worsened by my assumption that he was wanting to snack on rubbish before the dinner I had cooked.

'Okay,' he said. 'I'll take some eggs instead.'

Despite this rather weird response, I had no time to reflect on it before racing off to work. When I finished seeing my hospital patients, I was supposed to attend another work meeting but an uneasy feeling told me to go home instead. When I arrived, Abdul was nowhere to be seen and Toby was upset but would not talk to me. After I washed up and cleaned the kitchen, I sat down at the table, wondering about the boys.

At about 9 p.m., Abdul came into the kitchen and was still avoiding eye contact. I said, 'Hello again, Abdul!' in a cheerful voice, but he did not respond.

'I have a name, you know,' I snapped.

'I'm tired of hearing this. You're giving me a headache,' he shot back.

Neither of us should have continued the conversation, but we did, and it quickly escalated into Abdul threatening to leave home. The front door slammed shut and he stormed off into the darkness. I didn't wait up this time; I had already stayed up to all hours at other times, and tonight I needed my sleep.

When Abdul didn't show up for breakfast, I checked on him just before leaving for work. There was a lump in the middle of his bed and I could tell he was awake because when I put my hand on the shoulder part of the lump he stiffened. I gave him a hug.

'I'm so sorry how things were last night. I was too rough on you.'

No answer.

'Abdul, I want to make sure that you're okay.'

After another long pause, his shoulder relaxed and he wriggled himself out of the covers. His hoodie was still on and he shied away. Gently, with both hands, I turned his face towards me. Abdul's right eye was so bruised and swollen that it was almost shut. He had scratches and gouges over his forehead and cheek, and his left ear was swollen. He stared back at me, not saying a word. I soon discovered that he also had bruises and scratches down his back and legs. In that sickening moment, it became clear why he had had his hoodie up the night before and why he had been avoiding me. It also explained the eggs—he wanted to use them for the bruising around his eyes.

This is why Toby had been upset, too. He'd been put into a difficult situation: torn between following Abdul's instructions not to tell me, and his common sense, which told him that Mum should know. I decided to leave this issue for later that day and focused on Abdul.

After some persuading, Abdul told me quietly, 'I was beaten up.'

The day before, after school, three teenage boys had accosted him. Abdul and I had previously discussed two of them because they had a reputation at school of bullying and physical intimidation. In fact, Abdul had already been asked by the school to make a statement about an incident involving them that he had witnessed.

'You can't let them get away with this,' I said. 'We need to tell the police.'

Abdul refused my entreaties to involve the police. He also refused to tell the school and he also refused to see a doctor, even though I was certain he had broken a rib.

'I don't want to get them into trouble,' he said. 'I'll talk to them and sort it out myself.'

This last part worried me intensely. It was too big an issue for Abdul to deal with on his own, especially after everything he had been through. I was also worried that if things got out of hand, and accusations were made against Abdul, it could be an excuse for his bridging visa to be revoked. On this visa, Abdul can be re-detained at any time if a public servant in Border Force or a politician decides he is not of 'good character' or if they feel he has engaged in behaviour that is 'disruptive', or 'antisocial'. A simple accusation could have sent Abdul back to detention.

It was a dangerous situation, which is why, despite his wishes, I went straight to the school to talk to the deputy principal. I needed him to persuade Abdul to press charges against these boys and then allow the justice system to work.

When the deputy principal was certain that the assault did take place on school grounds, he promised to talk with Abdul later that day.

When he got home that afternoon, Abdul growled, 'You told the school, didn't you?'

Although he was annoyed, I could sense some relief in him. He explained that in Afghanistan there was not much law and order and so he was not confident that the police here would be able to do much. Abdul also worried that they might be too heavy-handed with the boys who beat him up. After almost two hours, I was able to persuade him that his attackers would be safe and that his speaking up could protect other students. We drove into the police station.

We had to wait a long time, watching the business of a busy Thursday evening pass through, but neither of us minded because it was clear that the police took his concerns seriously. We were given tea in paper cups and escorted into the clean but sparse interview room. The interviewing senior constable was calm, grounded and methodical. She cared, not only that Abdul had been assaulted but about his wider social wellbeing. I felt reassured that we had done the right thing. But even her presence did not spare me from what I was about to hear.

Abdul spent three hours giving his statement. Listening to what happened to him was one of the hardest things I've had to endure. The assault was prolonged and much worse than I had first thought. My heart ached as he recounted the racist words used against him. Abdul told the police officer how the muscle-bound, experienced brawlers took turns to beat him, while the other two held him down. She recorded the statement blow by blow. Abdul explained that he was aware that they were deliberately aiming for his jaw, trying to knock him out. They also tried to drag him down to the lake beside the school. God knows what would have happened if they'd managed it.

The attack would have been so much worse if Abdul had not had training in wrestling and boxing. Those hours in the gym in Afghanistan probably saved his life. The attack also gave me more understanding of why that training was necessary for a boy living in Afghanistan.

Abdul is a gentle boy, and during the attack he was concerned that his attackers, all so much bigger than him and two of them in the year above, might have been under eighteen. Because he was a few months older, and now over eighteen himself, he didn't want to engage in what he thought of as child abuse by fighting back. At one point, Abdul explained, he grabbed hold of one assailant and used him as a shield against the blows of the others. I can't imagine the restraint he must have needed during the ordeal.

Before we left, the senior constable suggested to Abdul that he might like to join some of the Police Citizens Youth Club (PCYC) programs. She followed up on these suggestions, with a stream of letters and invites to the PCYC and refugee support organisations arriving in the mail in the weeks that followed the attack.

I was convinced that this police officer's kindly and professional approach would become a cornerstone of Abdul's understanding of what living in a safe society with the rule of law was like. I believe these positive interactions with the police are the building blocks of community trust, safety and cooperation.

xxxxxxx

For some time afterwards, I tried to remain confident in the justice process for Abdul's sake, but his attackers remained at school, smirking at him in the courtyard. One of them even 'invited' him outside again. All Abdul could see was that his attackers had gotten off without any consequences. It seemed so unfair and erased all the good work that had been done in the police station.

I understood that this was primarily a police matter, but these bullies were interfering with another's right to learn, and I felt the school needed to do more regarding appropriate consequences for their actions. Prepping myself all day to be restrained and civilised, I met with the school principal and asked him how having these violent adolescents at the school helped to create a positive and safe learning environment for every other student? The principal explained that he could not expel or even give these boys detention because only the education department could do that, and only after the police matters were settled. He reassured me that the teachers were all aware of what had happened and there was a concerted effort by the school to keep these boys away from Abdul. He also indicated that Abdul was popular with other students and that he had himself noticed that Abdul was a peace-maker.

Abdul was in pain for weeks and his shoulder surgery recovery had been set back months. Yet Abdul was stuck seeing these taunting assailants every day with no ramifications for them. I could see he was becoming frustrated and at one stage expressed a wish to talk to them 'in their own language'. This idea, I suspect, was born of his fear, but I was afraid that if Abdul raised a finger, or even his voice, the consequences could be dire for him.

The adolescent brain has many positive attributes. For Abdul, these included being fervently passionate in his belief in justice and truth, and the fact that he was fearless in the face of risk. The downside for Abdul, as it is for many other adolescent boys, is that he thought he was ten feet tall and bulletproof.

In reality, Abdul was never going to do anything to these boys. He was letting off steam, but I got angry. I explained the risks of him being locked up again, but it did not further my case with the most stubborn person I know. Before too long, Abdul and I were arguing again, the reasoning parts of both of our brains shut off by emotion. I know I should have just shut up and listened, and I know what Abdul really needed through all this was love and comfort and not advice. But I couldn't stop because I was scared. It was too much of a reminder of what could happen to Abdul if his refugee application was rejected. He could be locked up with worse criminals than these teenage thugs and sent back to more injustice and violence in Afghanistan. It was all too hard.

What a wasted chance it all was.

After the interview, Abdul heard nothing more about the assault, but a year later we would read in the *Canberra Times* and then court reports that two of his attackers went on to commit more seriously violent crimes and are now in jail.

Chapter 46

LANGUAGE

Even when Abdul had just begun to learn English, I never felt that our language differences stopped us from understanding each other. Our intention to connect, and the rhythm of our discussions, were like a dance, the meaning carried despite the poor internet connection or scratchy phone lines. I didn't make my English too simple or too easy because that can change meanings. I wanted to give Abdul a challenge.

Abdul tells me that he remembers not just each new English word he encounters but also the context of when he learned the word. While in detention, he amassed a huge collection of small notebooks in which he wrote every new word he discovered. Each page of these worn notebooks is neatly filled with a hodgepodge of English words and their Dari translations.

In the months after moving in with us, Abdul's English improved exponentially. I know at first he couldn't fully understand our dinner-table conversations because sometimes his smiling and nodding were misplaced. Sometimes we slowed down for him, but mostly we felt the best thing to do was to push on. We had faith in Abdul's and Ahad's ability to learn.

Rob, whose second language is English, joked to Abdul that, 'You know your English is good when people stop saying that your English is good.'

Perhaps our Abdul was a little too precocious and cheeky in his English language classes. Like the day his Year Eleven English teacher was discussing the concept of homonyms—words that have the same spelling and pronunciation but different meanings. She asked the class, 'What about the word "date"? How many meanings does date have?'

The class suggested three meanings. Then Abdul interjected, 'No, Miss, there are four meanings.'

I can imagine his teacher sighing inwardly but pressing on.

'Abdul, I think there are only three, but what are you thinking?'

'Well, there is "date" on the calendar, "date" that you eat and "date" you take your girlfriend on. But there is also "date" meaning arsehole.'

The class erupted. Chaos ensued. From that day the word 'date' had its renaissance at his school.

Human language is not just words but also the dance *between* words. The way words are used conveys different levels of meaning. Words serve to mark differences in status, relationships, and between formal and familiar.

When Rob and I visited Hungary, the locals smiled indulgently at Rob when he slipped up and used the informal language small children do with their parents. Language can also give clues to a person's process in dealing with psychological distress. Sometimes a grieving person who has not fully resolved their loss will talk of their loved one in the present tense. Direct translation of mere words can never cover every nuance.

The Australian mode of communicating is, on the whole, far more direct than many others, and can seem abrupt or even rude to some. The answer to a question, 'Would you like to come shopping with me?' can lead to a long, complicated and frequently baffling conversation with Abdul. I don't know if it is his 'Afghanness' that is responsible or his own uncertainty. Despite pleading for a straightforward yes or no, Abdul will often give me a 'perhaps' or 'maybe'. Usually in the translation this means 'no', but I am still never too sure.

Recently I texted Abdul: *If you want to join me, I will spend most of the day at the coffee shop writing. You could do your Maths. Yay! Exciting life!*

Please note the lack of a direct question. Indeed, I am learning from Abdul!

His reply: *Noiceeeeeeeeeee*

See? Really, what does that even mean?

And sometimes Australian English, in its directness and cheekiness (translation: *rudeness*), can be interpreted by Abdul as too critical or disparaging. In Afghan culture, this can tap into considerations about the importance of saving face.

Surprisingly, the everyday phrase 'thank you', which is sprinkled around liberally in Australia, has provided one of the biggest challenges for us.

It had been bugging me that after months of doing things for Abdul, such as taking him to the doctor, driving him around or travelling across town to buy him the brand of dates he liked, he hadn't said a simple 'thank you'. In truth, I felt that I was being taken for granted.

Abdul explained that he did not think a verbal 'thank you' was needed for the things that I did. In his world, these things were what family did for each other. No need for thanks. I explained that I would like a 'thank you' because it was what I was culturally used to and it was expected in our family.

'A little appreciation goes a long way,' I told him, and it was also good practice for dealing with other Australians.

Abdul took offence and went on the defensive, which for him meant a huge push back. Within a short time, things were getting a bit out of hand and I understood that we weren't talking about small social transactions anymore.

'And where would we stop?' he retorted. 'Do I have to thank you for everything for the rest of my life?'

'Yes, mate, actually you do.' Abdul was fuming but I continued. 'I don't need or want thanks for doing the big things. I don't demand the other boys tell me "Thank you, Mummy, for giving birth to me" every day. Of course I don't. But, Abdul, I would like thanks for taking your washing in.'

We were as stubborn as each other and this was turning into one of those arguments that was going nowhere. Probably

Abdul was feeling he was being coerced into saying 'thank you' and he does not *do* coercion. His final response was that from now on he would refuse to thank me for anything.

So much for our wonderful intuitive understanding.

Almost a year after this conversation, Abdul started saying 'thank you' to me for small things. But I was still curious about having a cultural understanding of this dilemma so in a calm moment when Abdul's Hazara friend, Irshad, was visiting, I asked him about it.

Maybe because both of us were watching him intently, Irshad could tell something was up. He offered, 'Uh . . . whatever he says,' smiling at Abdul.

'Uh, Irshad,' I replied, 'I want to know from you. How do you say thank you?'

'*Tashakor.*'

'But in what circumstances do you say it?'

'If it is a big thing, you might say something like, "I hope you stay happy, have a good life," or "I hope you stay alive, your spirit." Another way of saying this in Afghanistan is: "I hope your hand doesn't get sore." Otherwise you just say *tashakor.*'

So we were back to square one.

It's not necessarily the words in language that tie us up in knots. It's the fact that the most important things are sometimes the hardest things to say. The truth is, this issue of 'thank you' was covering a much deeper ache around language: my name.

Chapter 47

THE EMMA AND ABDUL SHOW

The connection I have with my sons started before they were born. That is something special only a mother can have. The hours spent in perfect contentment, body curled around a sleeping Jasper, my face resting on top of his head, feeling his silky hair on the edge of my lips and breathing in that beautiful, warm baby scent. The powerful force of love that got me through the intense pain of infections when I needed to breastfeed Lucas. The joy I rediscovered in the happy fuss and snuggle of feeding my beautiful baby, once those difficult weeks were over. And Toby, contentedly tapping his sticky hands on my chest and playing with my hair as he was cradled in my arms. We have a language that doesn't always need words.

Abdul and Ahad had that connection with their mother, which has meant they've connected with me in a different way. But our love is still there. We just need to be clear and careful with each other because we communicate in so many different ways.

Between teenagers and their parents there is the issue of control. My boys want to make their mark on the world and lead their lives in their own way, while Rob and I are invested in them having happy lives in the long term and keeping them safe in the short term. All young people will make mistakes—most of them are not disastrous. Kids do need guidance, which means taking a bit of control. But I also know that if us parents try to prevent every bad thing from happening our kids will end up suffocated. This also means that parents often have to live with a great deal of anxiety. For Abdul, regaining a sense of control has been crucial for him, but keeping this balance has also been difficult for us to manage when working as a family.

The opposite of control is chaos and fate. Some people, especially those whose lives have been comfortable, scoff at the idea of fate, claiming we make our own destinies. The corollary of this must be that everything is under our control. But it isn't, and for someone who has come from a place of war, with all its hazards and unpredictability, the illusion of one's own control evaporates.

In detention, everything was controlled. Every step since has been a different form of limbo. Would Abdul be able to leave Darwin? Now he was worrying if he would be accepted as a refugee or if he would be deported. When would this decision be made? If he got a visa, what would happen in three or five years' time? Opportunities for a career path, a serious relationship and children, buying a house and building a future were not things Abdul could dream about in the same way Ahad, with permanent residency, or my other boys, could. It is so unfair that such an adventurous person had his autonomy cut off for so long.

Sometimes it seems that Abdul packs up all the anger, fear and frustration he has felt since leaving Afghanistan and throws it at me. Of course this is irrational and unfair, but this defence against difficult emotions, directing them to those who are safest, is common to us all. I joke that Abdul sometimes sees me as a combination of Daesh, Pauline Hanson and the worst of our politicians imprisoning kids, but when I feel his anger for them now directed at me it isn't a joke anymore. When Abdul is in this dark place he has frequently convinced himself that I have told him to leave. I suspect he thinks that I don't love him or that he is not important to me. In these states, he can't see that we care for him and it seems that he pushes the boundaries to see how safe he is. Sometimes we have pushed each other too far.

XXXXXXX

One incident we now call the 61,580 steps started like this. The whole family had been away at the coast for a week. Abdul and I were the last to leave the holiday house after the others had gone—six of us and two dogs mean that we are now a two-car family. While Abdul slept in that morning, Rob and I had spent several hours scrubbing, wiping and sweeping, and carrying and cramming bags and boxes into the car, before Rob took off with the other boys, who had helped 'a little'. After he had a leisurely breakfast, I asked Abdul to vacuum the upstairs room. By 11 a.m., I was overheated and gritty, but a coffee break was not going to happen until we finished the job and could drive somewhere because everything had been packed up.

When I went upstairs to check on progress, I found that Abdul had done nothing. The head of the vacuum had become blocked and he was just sitting there. He told me that he was waiting for me to come to fix it. Low blood sugar and the resentment that I'd done nearly all of the work made me snappy. His inertia made me even snappier.

Neither Abdul nor Ahad accept me raising my voice. Even a quiet rebuke will have them accusing me of yelling, and they seem to think that gives them some sort of free pass at righteousness. I can get pretty wound up and angry and I do raise my voice, and I also swear, but only to emphasise the message, such as 'I am *bloody-well* sick of doing all the work.' The expletive is never directed *at* them.

That morning Abdul responded by sitting on the grass outside for another hour while I finished the work on my own. Shutting me out as if I didn't exist is not a better way of arguing, and it is certainly not kind. Rather than easing the situation, I've found the silent treatment can prolong the tension and unhappiness for days.

Abdul continued his silence on the drive home. We stopped at the next town and he replied with more silence when I offered to buy him coffee and cake. Because it was after midday and he needed to eat, I suggested he buy something from another cafe and left him some money. When I returned, I saw that he had remained sitting in the hot car with the money still in his lap. I had to remind myself that he was not a dog or a baby and I would not be in trouble from the RSPCA or Child Protection. His stubbornness is truly remarkable and, despite being cross with him, I smiled.

But facing another hour of this treatment on the drive home made my chest tight. I wanted to clear the air and for us to be friends again so I apologised for speaking harshly and tried to engage Abdul in conversation. I told him I loved him. I explained to him about the amount of work I had done and how much I resented it when he didn't help me and that was why I snapped at him.

Throughout this monologue, Abdul had his whole body twisted away from me towards the window and had not once responded. When I asked, 'Abdul, what do you think?' he continued to say nothing.

Sadly—as happens with one-way conversations—I escalated my response and ended up blurting out what I was really thinking, which was an entire inventory of my resentments from the other times I'd been left by him and the boys to do things on my own.

Now Abdul turned around and said, 'Rob does the cooking, you don't. We have a cleaner. You don't even clean. I wash my own clothes and look after my own room. It is you who doesn't do a thing for the family. All you do is complain. You do nothing. You've never done anything. You just think you do.'

I drove on for a few more minutes, but soon realised I'd had enough. I had reached an emotional crashing point and was worried about driving in this state. I remembered how, when Abdul was still in detention, I'd told him that I was looking forward to us having some arguments because being too good and compliant indicates that a person does not feel entirely at home. But I had never expected this intensity.

'Okay, then. If I am such a bloody bitch, why are you taking a lift from me?'

'I don't need anything from you.'

'Is your phone charged?' I asked.

'Yes?'

'Good.' I pulled up by the side of the road. 'Get out.'

A look of surprise crossed his face.

'Get out then,' I said. 'If you hate me so much, get out and walk. I don't want to risk my life driving like this. If you don't need me, my kids do. If you can't even be fucking *kind*, you can walk, or you can call your friends. They're clearly much nicer people than me so get them to give you a lift.'

On a hot summer's day, 49 kilometres from home at a small town called Bungendore, Abdul got out of the car and I drove off. I did not go back to find him because from experience I knew he would not have backed down even if I had pulled the car onto the side of the road and spent hours pleading with him. It was a dramatic step, but I didn't think it was a risky one. It was daytime, Abdul was street-smart and very fit. He had a mobile phone, some money, a bus pass, and a school friend living nearby he could call on if he needed them.

Me taking that step—to drive safely and be around for my kids—reset my priorities. I was firm on my limits for him. When I got home, after a much more peaceful drive, I told

Rob what I had done. He looked at me, quiet, then put his arms around me.

'You did the right thing. These boys, I mean all of our boys, don't think about the big picture. They're all little buggers.'

'They aren't little buggers, they're quite big buggers, actually.' I giggled between tears and relief.

'I worry about you,' Rob said. 'I'll have a quiet man-to-man talk with him when he comes home.'

This 'I worry about you' was a glimpse of what Rob and I used to have. I realised how much it was costing to carry this load on my own.

Later that night, Abdul returned. He had walked the whole way, counting 61,580 steps on his phone app before it ran out of charge. He also took a photograph of himself kicking a brown snake and showed it to Toby, who he knew would tell me and get me worried. I later discovered that the snake in question was dead.

'Why didn't you call a friend?' I asked.

'I don't need anyone,' he insisted. But the break in his voice gave him away.

We have talked about this incident since. Our conclusion is that we are both very stubborn. Abdul's determination allowed him to survive in indefinite immigration detention that breaks nearly everyone else. My dogged refusal to back down or give up over the last few years means we are now a family. But he still ends these arguments with glassy eyes and the words 'I don't need anyone.'

XXXXXXX

During the writing of this book, I gave all my boys evolving versions of the manuscript to read and comment on. One winter afternoon, sitting in front of the fireplace and fortified with mugs of hot tea, Abdul gave me his feedback. Respecting his wishes, I removed several chapters because he thought they might seem disrespectful to the guards and other staff at immigration and he didn't want to contaminate the good work of many others he had encountered in the detention centre.

One of these deleted stories described a woman working in the detention centre who Abdul and many of the other unaccompanied children still call 'Mama'. When I discovered he was still calling her this on Facebook, I felt hurt and betrayed because Abdul has not called me by any name at all. I have not asked to be called Mum because Abdul will only ever have one mother. But he doesn't call me anything—not even Emma. I have no name. This breaks my heart if I dwell on it, as it did again that night as Abdul and I spoke about the book.

Sometimes I struggle to know what my place is in his life. The only role I have ever officially had with Abdul as far as immigration was concerned was a 'custodian' for community detention. They never expected me to care, and it was never seen as a fostering arrangement. I have not been offered, nor have I ever asked for, one cent from the government during our care of Abdul. We brought him into our family because we cared, and as far as I am concerned we are family.

Like many sources of pain, I had a compulsion to pick at the issue of 'Mama', even if it made it worse. As we spoke that afternoon, I realised that we were getting back into this old cycle of hurt. We had both tried to resolve the name issue so many times, but it still ended in arguments and tears.

'Of course I'm jealous of Mama,' I said. 'She's got a name. And she got paid to do the job she had. I don't see her calling you now or visiting. I've tried so hard and care so much, and it hurts that you still refuse to call me anything. How can I not think that I'm nothing to you? Every single other person has a name. Can't you see that?'

Abdul responded by defending this woman once again. 'You weren't there. It is none of your business. You don't understand and you're only telling your side of the story.' He wouldn't acknowledge my hurt.

'But, Abdul, it's a memoir, of course it's *my side*! I try to understand. I really do. But when I ask why everyone else in your life has a name, you just get angry.'

'Well, it is hard for me and you don't try to make it easier.'

The argument had now reached the red zone. I reacted angrily.

'Really? I don't try? For fuck's sake, I try all the time! I even put up with you calling me "Banana" because you thought that would help. I put my dignity on the line to help you and you don't lift a finger.'

And because I said 'fuck', he accused me of swearing at him. 'I never swear at you,' he said, which was true.

So in this space, on the woollen rug, which had turned into a fighting rink, he listed the many horrible things I had done to him.

'On my second day here, you told me you were going to kick me out of the car.'

I didn't recall this—all I remembered of his first week was happiness and a protective tenderness. I remembered driving him around, taking him to places, wondering if he was enjoying himself, trying, really trying, to communicate, which had been hard because he was so docile and agreed to everything. Perhaps I had said it, but I couldn't imagine having ever made this as a threat. Language had been difficult back then. I was so sad that all this time he'd carried around this misperception. No wonder he was upset with me.

'You say in this book that you are so proud of your boys for having let us into their lives. Well, it was hard for me too.'

He told me when he moved in with us that he felt out of place and lonely, and the language barrier created a distance. He told me that he hadn't wanted to stay and I thought back to all the times at the dinner table when he had been so quiet and seemed so meek.

Now that things were better in day-to-day life, I often forgot the Abdul of the first few months. But, of course, he hasn't. That afternoon, as we talked about the first draft of my book, misunderstandings and emotions abounded. Abdul angrily ripped into me again.

'You really hurt my shoulder that day, you know,' he said.

I knew he was talking about the supermarket incident, but I remembered it as an accident, not malevolence. Abdul, Toby and I had been doing the grocery shopping. It had been a long day and I was tired. In normal circumstances, I could have handled Toby on his own, but he was whirling into crazy excitement with Abdul, who was encouraging him to muck up. The boys were noisily running up and down the aisles of the supermarket, loading the shopping cart with stupid things, or running off with the cart just as I was about to put something in it. Basically, they were doing everything they could to make my shopping a challenge. At first, I tried to pacify them. Then I warned them through gritted teeth. When that failed, I did the death stare, but that was ignored too. Things were getting crazier so I tried with Abdul again, but he just stared back with a silly blank grin.

I had been sensing disapproval from the other shoppers. With my tear ducts stinging, what I really wanted to do was run away. With little kids, it is easier to do. You can put them under your arm and just leave. But with two big boys, and a week's worth of groceries to do, I felt cornered. This wasn't the first time he had goaded me to tears and I thought my distress would stop him—instead he kept going.

The next time Abdul sped past me down the aisle, I grabbed at his arm to contain him. It was only a few weeks after his shoulder surgery and the pain must have been immense because he crumpled to the ground. Appalled at what I had done, I immediately apologised, but he wouldn't listen. In his eyes, I had assaulted him and that was that. I couldn't believe that after all this time Abdul still thought I had done this deliberately.

Then, as we sat together on the rug, he brought up an incident involving Jasper.

'You made it like Ahad and I were the rude ones that night because we stayed up talking even though Jasper wanted to sleep,' he said. 'But you were the one who was angry and upset with Jasper and you gave him the finger when his back was turned.'

This was another chapter I wanted to forget.

'Yes,' I replied, chest constricted, eyes downcast with shame. 'I did.' I had been unfair to my own son.

It had happened in February 2015, the first weekend that Ahad came to live with us. I was so anxious that everything should go well that I had little tolerance for dissent. So when Jasper came down at 11 p.m. that first night of the reunion and asked us to be quieter so he could sleep, I asked him to be a bit more accommodating. Jasper argued back and I retaliated with, 'Just suck it up, don't be so precious.' We glared at each other, then Jasper stomped out.

I knew I had been disrespectful and unfair to my son, who was well within his rights to speak up. To make matters worse, very late that same night, when I heard Abdul and Ahad continuing to talk in their bedroom, I panicked that this was turning into a horrible dynamic where the boys would play me off against each other. I lost my perspective and lost my temper with everyone.

Another time, regrettably, I responded to Abdul during an argument with: 'Well, if you don't care, just fuck off and leave.' I meant he should give me some space, but instead he packed his bags and left. It took a week for me to find him and convince him to come home. It was a distressing time. We all missed him terribly, Toby especially. I couldn't call the police, as he wasn't exactly a missing person, and if immigration found out it could have been enough excuse for them to revoke his bridging visa and put him back in detention.

Instead I put out a call for help through Facebook and hoped that through these networks that some news would come through. Eventually he returned, having spent the week on a friend's couch.

Many times Abdul has packed his bags and many times I have been up most of the night pleading with him to stay. I am scared that he will leave our lives in the same heart-breaking way Ahad did and never come back. Abdul does not know that his running away also triggers a much deeper fear in me: of the few patients of mine who have suicided, one person went missing off the ward before they were found, too late, by the police several hours later. When Abdul runs away, I can't help reliving these old feelings of horror and grief.

Jasper had been due to travel overseas (his first time on his own) during the mid-year holidays in 2016 and Abdul had been angry and rude to me that day. As I wanted our farewell dinner with my son to not be usurped by this drama, I informed Abdul that if he couldn't be nice, he shouldn't bother joining us for dinner. Abdul's response was to not eat with us for a week. The only proof of life we had during that time was the condensation on his bedroom window each morning.

I felt bad that Abdul had kept these grievances pent up all of this time, but also I felt sad that Abdul, and Ahad, could not see what a difficult job it had been for me. In trying to show my love and devotion to everyone, there were many times when I felt as if I had failed everyone. I felt I hadn't even learned anything in doing this.

I knew that Rob originally agreed to have Abdul and Ahad with us because, as a child of refugees, he had an understanding of the boys' predicament, but he also said 'yes' to them coming because he loved me and trusted my judgement. Both of us give all we can in our parenting of our three boys, but with Abdul and Ahad, Rob had a more 'hands off' approach. In my need to make all of this work because I saw it as my responsibility, I took on the additional hard yards as far as Abdul and Ahad were concerned in the realms of emotional input.

Rob, from the position of observer rather than participant, had taken to calling our arguments the 'Emma and Abdul show'. This didn't help. I suspected in his own way he was voicing some concern about the situation with the boys taking up my time and energy, but I would have preferred him to step in as he had always done with our own sons.

I had ended up depleted—and, as a result, a little resentful towards my husband. Both of us were becoming our own islands of distress. Of course, we had a notion of what was happening, but there were so many priorities eating into our time together (kids, work, other responsibilities) that we just persevered hoping that things would improve in the long run. At times, when I sat watching junk television by myself late at night, Rob stayed in his den, while on the weekend he developed an intense interest in keeping bees.

I wondered if we were going to make it.

If they only knew how much I loved them all.

XXXXXXX

When Abdul first came to Canberra he drew a picture of a mother and baby and gave it to me. This mother was wearing a headscarf. It is a puzzle to me that he has no name for me because otherwise he is affectionate. He wants to hang out with me, he leans against me when we are reading together, he pinches my cheek—an Afghan thing—and he sends me love heart emojis. All I want is to be special to him.

I wanted Abdul to be with our family not out of some solemn sense of obligation but because we were special to him and because we had a precious connection. Through my tears that afternoon, and in my spiral of crazy, catastrophic thinking, the hope that I held on to was that the reason he was this way towards me is that he was still struggling with these feelings, too.

xxxxxxx

The discussion about the book had taken hours. But this time by the end we were sitting side-by-side on the old woollen rug.

'Why do we argue and fight so much, Abdul?' I asked, my eyes still feeling tight and sore under swollen lids.

He shifted and readjusted his arm, which was draped around my shoulders. For the first time in many days, he looked into my eyes.

'Because we're afraid of the "what ifs".'

'What do you mean?'

'What if you don't care? What if I get sent away? What if . . .?' He stopped.

'Maybe we use too many words.'

He stretched over to turn on the kettle, which was on the ground, and soon we were sipping hot cardamom tea. Then he pinched my cheeks and smiled brightly.

'But I'm home now!'

xxxxxxx

Although it was getting late, we decided to go for a run together around the less developed East Basin of Lake Burley Griffin to clear the air and restore equilibrium.

We started in twilight near the palliative care hospice built on the lake's edge. The cold slapped us hard as we got out of the car, but the wet mist felt good on my sore eyes. After four days of solid rain, we slipped on the mud until we reached the bike path.

The warm light and clusters of people gathered quietly together in the hospice were reassuring. As we ran, I thought about the news feeds I'd been reading, describing what was happening to men, women and children in Afghanistan. They did not get to die in peace. In the hospice, the person and their loved ones were being looked after with care and kindness, which is the way it should be. I didn't share these thoughts with Abdul.

As we ran, we began to warm up, but never quite to the fingertips. We started having happier conversations; our running chats are usually absurd and puerile. Abdul put on his 'silly voice' and became excitable again. After the day's unhappiness, we were pushing our spirits to be high. Abdul burst into a Hazaragi song. I tried to join in for the 'Hah!' parts and when it was my turn I sang the Muppets 'Mahna

Mahna' song badly. Running like this is not a time for sweet singing; it is a time for belting out songs—or just yelling. In the wetlands part of the lake, with ponds and long reeds and waterbirds all around, we were alone so there was no need to worry about being heard.

We came to the well-lit restaurants along the lake fore-shore. This made us finally slow down and reminded us we were hungry. We sniffed the air with appreciation, breathing in the delicious aromas: the caramelly tomato and yeast of the pizzeria; the warm, creamy curry spice of the Indian restau-rant; the hops of the bar and charred steaks on a barbecue. Then we entered the dark again. The lake on our right was black and choppy with the rising wind and even though I couldn't see them I knew by their scent in the winter air that the plum trees had started blossoming. The promise of spring.

As we picked up our pace and raced across the bridge. Abdul exclaimed, 'Do you feel we are flying?'

I thought to myself, 'Yes, I do now, but how on earth do you drive me to distraction then have us laughing together so soon?'

We returned cold, wet and exhilarated, and ready to start another round of the Abdul and Emma show.

> Out beyond ideas of wrongdoing and rightdoing,
> there is a field. I'll meet you there.
>
> When the soul lies down in that grass,
> the world is too full to talk about.
> Ideas, language, even the phrase 'each other'
> doesn't make any sense.
>
> —Rumi

Chapter 48

ONE OF US

There were dark days in 2016, but Abdul is fundamentally an optimist who takes his happiness seriously. Sometimes he bursts into a spontaneous Afghan dance around the kitchen bench, flinging his arms wide and singing happy songs. He will grab my hands and stare into my eyes, playfully singing a language I do not understand, before spinning away in dance again. I have had to stop him jumping up on the bench because one of these days it will break.

The first time I heard Abdul speaking Hazaragi it gave me a shock. It's always the same with people you get to know 'in English' only to discover that they have this other language, one that you will likely never know. Perhaps it challenges the illusion that we can ever know another person completely. I remember this happened when Rob and I started dating.

I knew that he spoke Hungarian, but hearing him talk with his sister and father, and realising he had another world that I was not a part of, intrigued me.

I suspect that people who can speak more than one language have more appreciation of other cultural perspectives. Each language conveys information in a slightly different way and there are nuances in words that are not directly translatable. Many Aboriginal languages have been or are nearly lost, and sadly I have not learned even one yet. But I do know some words in Wiradjuri that have more meanings than any English word can convey. Such as *Yindyamarra*, which means doing things the right way, living respectfully; of doing things gently, kindly and slowly. *Ngurrumbang* means birthplace or home, but has a deeper meaning of connection to the land and environment. Language connects us to home, to culture, and to an understanding of the world and a way of being that can never be fully translatable.

Some years ago, when I arrived home from work one evening, I saw Rob at our kitchen bench preparing food for two dark-haired, well-dressed little boys. All three were nattering in Hungarian. Rob was different, too. He was standing straighter than usual, his tone of speech was more mannerly, and he even seemed to be serving the food more neatly. I felt as if I had entered a parallel universe. Where on earth were my scruffy blond children? It turned out that my boys were sprawled on the couch, hidden from view, and that these other boys, whose father was Hungarian, were their school friends. What I have observed is this: when people switch to their mother tongue, it is not only their language that changes.

Abdul and Ahad stand straighter and speak with a definite strength in Hazaragi. This is not just the confidence of speaking their own language but in their whole sense of being. I love listening to them. They even move differently. Language and ties to one's culture give strength.

Abdul and Ahad do not look like my boys, who are tall and lanky with unruly mops of wavy hair and big eyes. Or, as they helpfully correct me, 'Big eye *sockets*, Mum.' Abdul and Ahad are stocky rather than spare, with dark-almond eyes, dark hair and olive skin. I am short and strong, and darker-skinned than my children, so I am amused—and pleased—when people assume Abdul, Ahad and I are biologically related and comment on our similar smile.

We might be different in appearance, language, experience and religion, but for our family in Canberra such elements do not divide us. We all want the same things: love, connection and freedom. This is not limited to our small family, either. Arriving at Sydney airport after an overseas trip, it is always lovely to look around and realise that you can't tell if a person is Australian by looking at them or even listening to them. Australia is a multicultural society and I am proud of this. There is no one way to describe an Australian.

Identity and connection are more than waving a flag, too. Patriotism is more than a tribute to the brave young men and women who have sacrificed themselves in war. Maybe our Australian identity is recognising the connection we have to each other and also to our land. This place looks after us: the rocks, the soil and the shape of the earth. The trees and plants, the animals and birds, the way the sun falls on our skin or pushes through the clouds—all of this is what it means to be Australian. Our national identity can't be defined by one thing, not even a passport. Our identity and connection to each other and our environment is also the invisible thread that connects us all.

Chapter 49

A HORRIBLE REALISATION

Back in late 2015, as I was reading through Abdul's immigration documents to prepare for his Fast-Track interview, I found something bad. It happened back in 2014 when Abdul was still in detention, but it was only until towards the end of 2016 that life felt settled enough to confess to Abdul what I had found.

Back in 2014, my letters and entreaties on Abdul's behalf to the department must have been a small thorn in the minister's side. Scott Morrison, the then immigration minister, it seemed to me did not like the possibility of negative publicity (or, as they had written, 'possible media interest') and had personally ordered that Abdul be transferred to Nauru as soon as possible. Presumably he would be out of sight and out of reach from the media there as Nauru had not allowed journalists to visit. My efforts to help Abdul, it turned out, had almost caused him to be sent there.

I can't adequately describe the horrible realisation that my appeals to common sense and human kindness had backfired so dangerously, and how much I would have blamed myself had he been sent to Nauru. I felt a raw shame that my actions and naivety could have harmed Abdul.

Those who have never dealt with immigration might dismiss as irrational my earlier fears about the government's callous disregard for Abdul and all other asylum seekers. Here in Abdul's file, however, was proof that the government had indeed sunk to such unbelievably shameful depths that it would deport a minor to Nauru for reasons which could only be to prevent light being shed on that child's predicament.

The FOI paperwork included my letters to the minister appealing for Abdul on compassionate and medical grounds. In these letters, I gave my word that we would keep quiet about the whole process if only he could be released. I also offered our cooperation to be used as an example of the department's 'compassionate activities'. This offer, of course, was never taken up.

The original submission to the Department of Immigration for Morrison to consider was placement of Abdul in the community. It summarised information such as his arrival date and that he was a sixteen-year-old boy on his own. His serious medical and psychiatric conditions were recorded; notably, his IHMS medical notes that clearly indicated 'NOT for offshore processing/settlement' because of a 'history of torture and trauma'. The summary advised that 'the power to place him in the community resides with you as Minister for Immigration and Border Protection'.

The minister declined this humane approach and the handwritten comments adjacent to Morrison's signature were that 'arrangements should be made for Master (Abdul) to be transferred to Nauru once he receives a medical clearance'. This from his legal guardian who must have been aware what conditions on Nauru were like.

The emails included in Abdul's heavily redacted file told the story in a series of enquires about his medical progress. The reasons, it seems, that he could be sent to Nauru, shoulder surgery or not. The minister recommended Abdul's offshore transfer be expedited, and I read a series of emails between public servants in immigration working out how much damage would ensue without surgery or physiotherapy. There was no consideration of his mental health needs in this decision-making.

The reason that Morrison wanted to transport this vulnerable child to Nauru could only have been possible negative media interest and a major part of the submission consisted of media talking points just in case this became a public issue.

Of course, we were kept in the dark at the time. Now I wonder, if I had known what was happening back then, would it have stopped me? I can't know the answer for sure, but I think it is more likely that I would have fought back harder. The only option Abdul had was for me to keep trying—they were going to send him to Nauru regardless.

Luckily for Abdul, not all the public servants in immigration were mindlessly and ruthlessly grinding out the government's political agenda. There were guardian angels working for Abdul (and, I am sure, for many other asylum seekers and refugees) in the department. They were the ones who stood up for Abdul and who took the risk of allowing him to live with us. These kind and caring people have my unending gratitude.

Chapter 50

KINDNESS

Abdul and I were visiting Melbourne in the winter of 2016 and met with some of his friends from the detention centre at an Afghan restaurant. It was a cosy, homely place with rugs and textiles and knick-knacks on the walls. We stuffed ourselves with food, starting with *bolani*, the fried flatbread filled with potato, leek or pumpkin, followed by *mantu*, steamed meat dumplings, lamb and chicken kebabs, kofta meatballs, a spicy onion and lamb ragout called *dopiaza*, and a fragrant slow-cooked *qoorma* with chunks of eggplant, accompanied by mounds of cardamom rice and naan bread.

Our feast ended with traditional Afghan ice cream, which is surprisingly chewy, with an intensely creamy, almost musky taste. Some of us had a glass of shiraz, which Abdul's friend Sajad chose because he had lived in Shiraz as a refugee from

Afghanistan. The table was crowded with plates of food and our conversation was animated with challenging ideas and good humour.

Reza, with his dark hair slicked back into a ponytail and wearing a thick metal chain over his chunky knitted sweater, was the same age as Abdul. His family had arrived by boat from Iran and now he was looking forward to finishing school. I knew that Abdul found hanging out with Reza's family reassuring. I also knew that in the detention centre, despite all her burdens, Reza's mum had also kept a maternal eye out for Abdul. Reza was almost as cheeky as Abdul and they kept up a banter that was hard to follow. They were speaking English out of consideration for me—normally they would have spoken in variations of Persian.

I pointed out a Hungarian vase, which I thought was out of place in the restaurant. Looking closer, I found it was inscribed in Russian and I made a flippant comment that maybe one of the Russians who invaded Hungary took it with him when he afterwards invaded Afghanistan.

'They tried,' said Abdul, 'but like everyone else it didn't last.'

'Yeah, it's not Afghan,' said Reza with a mischievous smile for Abdul and Sajad, changing this potentially heavy subject, 'cos all the Afghan things are *brown*.'

Sajad was a more prudent and philosophical dinner guest. Given another set of circumstances, I could see him as a diplomat. Clean-cut, with a solid build, he was about ten years older than Abdul and Reza. He was an Afghan whose parents had escaped to Iran many years before. He had also been in the detention centre with his wife and their baby, who was born during their incarceration.

I could tell the restaurant owners were almost bursting at the seams trying to work out our connection to one another. One young Hazara man, an Iranian and another man who could possibly be from anywhere. And then there was me. When they finally asked, the men named the countries where they were born but none mentioned being a refugee or having been in detention. I sensed this touched a nerve and to deflect from further questions I asked the waiters where they thought I was from. Usually people guess Greek or Italian. They said Iranian. I'd never had this one before.

'Well, actually, I'm Koori.' I explained what that meant and, then, as I expected, the waiter pointed out that I was not that dark. I explained that just as when you add milk to tea, it is still tea—things such as colour do not alter identity. This usually changes the subject and it did this time, too.

As we got back to our own conversation, Sajad said that I was kind for what I had done for Abdul. The word *kind* describing *me*, rather than my actions, hit me hard. What did he mean by it? What he'd said made me awkward, for as well as finding it hard to accept compliments, nowadays it seems kindness is often misinterpreted as weakness and a liability. It's also a hard thing to live up to. I am kind sometimes, but I am also sometimes not kind.

Besides, we were way past kindness by then. The life I had built with Abdul and had tried to with Ahad had been hard work and a gut-wrenching, emotional roller-coaster. Mere kindness would not survive what we have been through. What we needed was courage and blood and endurance, which is how mothers love their children.

Yet Sajad was right. When I first met Abdul and Ahad, it was kindness, moral conviction and, certainly, pity that made me want to do something. How could seeing anyone in that dreadful situation not arouse pity? But this was not the truth now. The reason I continue with Abdul, and even with an absent Ahad, is love. It is still important to be kind, but this will only get you so far. Love is stronger and family is more than just blood.

xxxxxxx

Yet it is the kindness in these people—the asylum seekers who have been so poorly treated by the system—that is most remarkable. I have seen how Abdul's friends have looked out for him, and despite the treatment they have received in Australia, the kindness extended to us, his new family.

It made me think of another time, about a year earlier, when we had to visit Sydney for the day and Abdul wanted me to meet his friend Abbas. He and Abbas knew each other through wrestling in Kabul. Abbas certainly looked like a wrestler—his cauliflower ears were a clue, but even more of a clue was his muscular build, thick neck and the balanced and graceful way he carried himself. Abbas had arrived in Australia some years earlier and he tried hard to explain his situation to me in English. His visa meant that he was not allowed to work, volunteer or study. He existed on an allowance from the government, which I knew was less than the dole. He wanted to keep up with his wrestling training, but the gym fees were too expensive. He was lonely and bored, and frustrated because he wanted to work and to contribute.

Abbas showed us around Sydney Olympic Park and I deliberately lagged behind so the two young men could speak more comfortably in Hazaragi. We caught the train together to Merrylands and I felt a spark of recognition. This place reminded me of my childhood years in the Sydney suburb of Homebush forty years ago. The long, crowded suburban street of one- or two-storeyed shops. The almost sickly tropical scent of the fruit shops, the delicatessens, which to me, weirdly, smelt like bandaids, and the newsagents, which reminded me of puzzlebooks with pens that revealed the invisible-ink answers. Most of all, it was the diverse mix of people, speaking a multitude of languages, that brought me back, except this time rather than hearing Greek and Turkish I was hearing mostly Arabic and Mandarin mixed in with Australian accents.

Abbas took us to an Afghan restaurant, and as they walked through the door I sensed a change in both young men, an easing of a tension that I only noticed in its absence. Abdul clapped his hands together as he studied the menu. They excitedly strategised together about the feast we would have and reminisced about meals that were cooked for them at home. After we ate our fill of the generous portions, Abbas asked if anyone would like tea. I ordered a chai and some sweets, but no one else did. We sat for a bit longer, mostly because we couldn't move after so much food. As Abbas got up with his hand on his hip pocket, I stood up and brightly said,

'I'll shout'. Abdul shushed me and gestured for me to put my purse away. 'Abbas invited us so he wants to pay,' he insisted. 'Well, give him this,' I said, handing Abdul a fifty under the table. 'No!' he whispered back urgently. Abbas would be insulted.

So this asylum seeker used the few dollars he had to buy me, a rich doctor, lunch. I was a little embarrassed, but mostly I was honoured. I reflected on the kindness and generosity of this young man, who, if he had arrived just a few months later, would now tragically be on Manus Island, and whose desire to work and help our community here has not been allowed.

Chapter 51

THE WORST JUST KEEPS HAPPENING

It was Jasper's seventeenth birthday and it was lovely to watch him and Abdul sitting in our warm kitchen that winter's day sharing a pot of chai. They were playing, or, as they would prefer to call it, *building* electronics. I couldn't help reflecting that when Abdul turned seventeen he had been locked up in detention for nearly a year and a half. Jasper's life was ahead of him with promise and adventure, while Abdul still had no idea if, or when, he would ever be free.

That morning I had heard the news of yet another Daesh attack on Hazaras in Kabul. The Afghan government had decided to bypass sending a new electricity supply to the Bamiyan Province, which is one of the poorest provinces in the country and predominantly Hazara. This decision was widely seen as more evidence of ethnic discrimination and people were demonstrating. Two suicide bombers walked into the protest and set off their explosives, killing 80 people and injuring over 230 more. This toll would likely rise as more people died from their wounds in a health system that could not cope. No one would ever measure how many people had their lives ruined forever.

The news of this bombing was not particularly prominent in any Australian newspaper, just as most of the other regular bombings and murders of Hazaras in Afghanistan, Pakistan and Iran weren't. Whenever I heard these reports, though, I always wished they wouldn't call them 'suicide' bombers because the real intention was murder.

As I joined the boys that morning, I didn't say anything about this recent atrocity but instead gave each of the boys an extra-big hug. If Abdul didn't know, I didn't want to ruin his fun; if he did, maybe the distraction of play was needed.

Watching the boys in the safety of our kitchen, I still found it hard to imagine the situation Abdul had escaped from. Nothing would ever take away the awful memories and the horrific sights, sounds and smells that he was left with, and even though he was now in Australia the atrocities never stopped. It seemed that each time the Afghan boys checked their Facebook feeds there was more evidence of violence and genocide.

On the bad days, when he had that hollow-eyed look and I knew the ghosts of PTSD were again with him, I stayed vigilant. Usually it was because Abdul had heard more hideous news. He always tried hard to conceal what he had learned as he wanted to protect us as much as defend himself, but some days his anguish couldn't be hidden.

So, on that particular day, I thought I'd give Abdul a few hours of reprieve and let everyone enjoy Jasper's birthday.

Chapter 52

SEEING REFUGEES ON BOATS

There was a place in Canberra that I had never mentioned to Abdul. After a week of terrible stories about what was happening to the people on Nauru and Manus Island, Abdul expressed his belief that no one in Australia cared. I understood why he felt that way and I thought that perhaps it was time to show him something.

The *SIEV X* memorial was a community project to remember one of the most terrible maritime disasters to beset people trying to reach Australia. Of the 421 refugees who set off from Sumatra in Indonesia in October 2001, 353 people drowned when this horrendously overcrowded twenty-metre boat sank in a storm off Java. One hundred and forty-six of the dead were children. SIEV is a government abbreviation for Suspected Illegal Entry Vessel. It seems to me that even in death these people do not get a break from words designed to manipulate meaning.

Weston Park is a quiet place on a peninsula of Lake Burley Griffin dotted with towering eucalypts and groves of oaks and evergreen trees. On this shiny-blue spring day in late 2016, families were picnicking on the grass under pink-blossomed plum trees. From the lake's edge, meandering up the hill, were 353 white poles set body-lengths apart: a pole for each soul lost.

There were tall ones for adults and shorter ones for children, and while some had the person's name and age written on them, over half were sadly unnamed. None bore portraits. A school, church, parish or community had sponsored each of the poles and each had its own unique artwork painted or carved into it. Many featured butterflies, doves, flowers, or Australian bush or rural scenes, and many were painted with pictures of children playing with soccer balls or kites.

It was a heartbreaking experience to walk past post after post. Many of the deceased were family groups, all drowned. Closest to the water, almost cast adrift, was a small pole, and pointlessly I found myself worrying about this baby so close to the water. I saw the names of children, now lost to the world, who would have been the same age as Abdul and Ahad. They could have been on this boat in the dark, angry ocean that night.

Before Abdul came out of detention, I was trawling through the internet trying to see if there were any pictures of his boat or of Abdul himself because I was trying to understand his journey. I was also forgetting what he looked like. I found a video made by a passenger on a dilapidated Indonesian fishing boat just like the *SIEV X*. In this video, it was also a bright-blue day and you could sense the wind whipping by, and in the background was the loud rumble of the boat engine. Many on the top deck were young and middle-aged men, but underneath I could see the forms of women and some small children covered with blue and black tarpaulins and the occasional orange life vest. As the camera panned around, the passengers' faces were listless and empty: they knew they still needed to survive this dangerous journey before any dreams of safety and happiness could begin.

A year after he came to us, Abdul showed the same video to me, and I was shocked to discover that this had been his boat. It is horrible to see these images of unknown people on refugee boats and even worse to think about someone you love facing the same perils. Abdul had sat on top of a petrol drum on the side of the boat because there was no room anywhere else, which is why he wasn't visible in the video. It had been made on the first day, he said, because afterwards everyone was too seasick to film. On the second and third day, it was stormy, with high seas, and the boat had been violently tossed by waves as huge as walls. Everyone clung on to whatever they could, terrified: like Abdul, they could not swim. If Abdul, my brave boy, says something is scary, then I know I should believe it. He told me he stayed put on that drum, not moving and not sleeping, for three and a half days.

On the fourth day, the boat was intercepted by the Australian Navy and everyone was made to sit bunched together on the back of the patrol ship. As Abdul was loaded on to the ship, he was preoccupied with worry that one of his legs would have to be amputated: after not moving for three days, he could no longer feel it. The Navy gave each of the passengers a tiny bit of boiled rice. People weren't allowed to use the toilets below and Abdul described people having to piss and shit off the edge of the boat. Abdul was sprayed with other people's excrement, but he didn't complain because what could anyone do? They had to do it somewhere. When he got off at Christmas Island, his first thought was to get clean again.

That Ahad and Abdul both survived is nothing but luck. A few weeks before Abdul set off from Afghanistan in 2013, one of these refugee boats, with at least 55 people on board, sank within seven kilometres of Australia's interception zone and within easy reach of Australian patrol boats. The government's explanation that the boat was in 'no distress' was inconsistent with the concerns of customs surveillance officers who noted that the vessel appeared to be 'dead in the water'. Sadly, after a Navy patrol boat sent out later could not find the vessel, the rescue coordination centre of the Australian Maritime Safety Authority (AMSA) declined to mount a search and rescue effort until debris was sighted. Eventually, when the boat was found capsized, only thirteen bodies were recovered. There were no survivors.

A few months after Ahad got on to his boat, another boat sank. On 17 December 2011, the *Barokah*, carrying around 250 people, sank 40 nautical miles from Indonesia. That evening, a local fishing boat managed to rescue 34 people and sent distress calls to Australian authorities, who forwarded the messages to Indonesia. In turn, Indonesian's search and rescue agency, BASARNAS, asked Australia to help coordinate the rescue response. AMSA refused and neither country did anything for two days. Over 200 people drowned.

Most of the ocean between Indonesia and Christmas Island is covered by BASARNAS, which is insufficiently resourced to cover rescues for this vast area. Rather than the Australian government improving communication and assisting the Indonesians, it appears that in many cases the Australian response has been to do little. Because of this inaction from both countries, lives have been lost.

The data is elusive, but the most reliable research from Monash University's Australian Border Deaths Database suggests that between January 2000 and November 2017 around 2000 people drowned on their journey to Australia. Rather than practical and prudent efforts, in cooperation with our closest neighbour, the Australian government is using this body count to justify offshore processing.

No one ever wants to see families risk their lives by crossing the oceans in a boat. But it must be understood that people do not undertake this dangerous journey for an easier life. Most, if not all, people who are refugees would rather not leave their homeland. They do it because they have to. Sending people to offshore prisons indefinitely and claiming to do this for safety reasons shows an appalling ignorance about what people and their children are facing every day and what they are willing to do to save their own lives.

The posts in the park marking the graves of those who died on the *SIEV X* offered a simple message of hope: we have not forgotten you. That others walking, jogging or on bicycles had stopped at this memorial to contemplate this loss was uplifting and reassuring. I saw a mother with her two school-aged children wipe tears away and an old man look before dropping his head. I placed my hand on these poles, closed my eyes against the tears, and offered my prayers. Abdul and I did not discuss the memorial on the drive home, but sat side-by-side in quiet thought. People cared then and they still care now. How can anyone not?

Chapter 53

LEILA AND ALI

There had been a couple in Darwin detention centre that understood what Abdul had been through and they had taken this unaccompanied teenage boy under their wings. Their names were Leila and Ali. Leila was the young mother so fiercely protective of her unborn baby that time I visited the detention centre and I have still never forgotten her words: 'They can call me illegal, but don't call my baby illegal.' Her husband, Ali, I remembered as a tall man who stood away from the group. He spoke little, and our language barrier meant we could not converse much, although I had seen how caring and protective he was of his pregnant wife.

Leila gave birth to Jubin, their first son, while still in detention. She was in the hospital for five days with guards outside her door the whole time. When the guards told the couple that immigration would not allow them to take a photo of their newborn baby, a kindly midwife brought in a camera in secret.

Abdul was besotted with this beautiful little baby and so proud of his friends who were now parents for the first time. I think it was possibly Jubin's birth, and all the care and attention he received from Leila and Ali, that kept Abdul from sliding into complete despair when he was in Darwin. When the family was finally released in 2015, we drove to see them. Despite not having seen Abdul for several months, little Jubin's face positively glowed when he recognised him. There was so much cheek-pinching and kissing and bouncing on the bed that I thought there was going to be some sort of accident. I had never witnessed a teenage boy so adoring of a baby.

During that visit, Leila said she thought of Abdul as family, a younger brother, and over the years since then she and Ali have supported Abdul from afar, including driving many hours to take him on an unscheduled holiday when tensions at home had become too great.

I heard news about the family from time to time from Abdul, including that Leila had had another baby, Farjad, but it was some time before I saw them again in 2017. Jubin was now three and Farjad was one. While Abdul and Ali were out helping a friend move house, I stayed with Leila and the children in their tiny flat, which backed on to a noisy road. Leila had made exquisite iced tea with saffron, rosewater and chia seeds and we sat and talked.

This is what I observed that afternoon with this lovely family. The children drape themselves over Leila while they study my face and listen to our adult conversation. Gradually

Jubin becomes more curious and we start to play together, which allows Leila some space to prepare dinner. Little Farjad pulls himself up on the lounge, keeping an eye on us the whole time. He is almost walking, but is still very cautious, and he looks to his mum for reassurance before approaching me.

Leila helps me understand what Jubin is saying as he shows me his toys. He is just learning English, which will be his third language. I can see that he is trying to teach me his toys' names. Jubin's play becomes more animated and we move on to a game where he sneaks up on me to launch himself into my arms exclaiming, 'Baby!' It is getting more hilarious and uproarious until Leila says a few quiet words to him that calm him down for a few moments—before he launches into the wild rumpus again with a cheeky twinkle in his eye.

Ali comes home with Abdul, both tired and work-stained from helping their friend. The two boys home in on Ali, excited and happy to see their dad. He scoops them up with delight, one on each arm, and carries them into the kitchen where he greets Leila, who smiles warmly back. Ali politely says hello to me and then excuses himself to have a shower. The boys follow him up the corridor and he calmly tells them to keep the door shut because guests are here. Abdul sits on the floor next to me and the little boys look at him shyly.

When Ali comes out a little while later, he looks after the boys' needs, including shuffling them, one by one, into their showers, and he juggles all of this while talking to us. Ali alternates between holding one of his sons while talking to the other, and then the other way around. Smoothly, comfortably and with beautiful warmth.

Leila signals to Ali and he passes Farjad into her arms. When Leila tucks her baby close to feed him the room becomes quieter.

Ali gives Jubin a drink from the fridge and we continue our conversation. Ali's English has improved significantly and I realise that his demeanour has softened and relaxed so much from when we first met. He now smiles readily and we have an engaged, wide-ranging chat.

Since leaving detention, Leila and Ali had been living an insecure existence on a bridging visa. Despite four years having passed since they arrived in Australia, they had not yet had their refugee claim assessed through the Fast-Track process. Ali told me that the department wanted more information, including, unbelievably, proof that their children were born in Australia. Despite being conceived and born here, their sons were also considered illegal maritime arrivals and were stateless, despite never having set foot in a boat.

Ali told me that he never had a chance to go to school, but he wanted to work as many hours as he could so that Leila, who had had a tertiary education, could study further, maybe in an allied health field. He values education and wants his children to have this chance, too. Since leaving detention, Ali had worked in factories and labouring jobs to provide for his family. But since the temporary bridging visa rules had changed, he was no longer allowed to work. Ali has some of his own dreams and showed us some exquisite woodworking projects that he would like to try in the future.

Despite their precarious position, Leila and Ali were using all their strengths to create hope and a future for their children. And as a couple, I know that theirs is a love story that I hope will one day be told. Their devotion to and respect for each other through their struggles is beyond doubt.

xxxxxxx

Leila and Ali are remarkable people. Their resilience in times of adversity has been exceptional. I'm certain others would struggle to survive as well if faced with the same challenges. Just think about what an amazing job they could do if they didn't have these everyday obstacles in Australia.

As a perinatal and infant psychiatrist, I know that protecting and strengthening that earliest relationship between parents and children not only leads to happier children and parents, and healthier emotional and cognitive development, but is also a preventative factor against mental illness, behavioural problems, learning difficulties and even later physical illness. The first 1000 days' movement in Australia and the rest of the world is an acknowledgement that from conception through to an infant's second birthday are the most crucial to a child's development. Experiences during this time, as well as nutrition, can have long-term consequences for a person's health and wellbeing. It is clear that a child's development in their first 1000 days is significantly affected by the physical and emotional environments of this period. Early stress, trauma and neglect can cause significant and permanent damage.

Sadly, what is being done by our government in the name of 'deterrence' flies in the face of all we know about child health and development. It is now well established that Australia's treatment of asylum seekers, especially children, has already caused long-lasting harm. The government can't say they didn't know at any step of the way. For years, every peak medical body in Australia has given their submissions about the harm that is being caused.

If we damage parents, we damage children. By the time refugees arrive here as parents, they are often at the limit of their capacities. Being locked up indefinitely further erodes those capacities. Even outside of detention centres, temporary visas prolong the stress and fear of being returned to the place that they had fled from. Instead we need to give parents security and hope; that way, it is passed on to their children.

Parents also need support. They need adequate resources to start their new lives here. To escape a war zone or persecution requires a great deal of courage, resourcefulness and endurance. It makes sense to get these people going again. Timely assessment of their claims for asylum, access to English classes, access to health care (especially mental health services), and support for accessing education will help refugees, and will also help us as a nation.

Refugees and their children also need our voices. They have no say in Australia. Only Australian citizens can vote to change these policies. With votes, the policy of detaining people on Nauru and Manus Island would stop, the policy of locking people in indefinite detention would stop, and we could give refugees permanent protection again so they could have solid hope of a future. What we need to do is to raise awareness of these issues and tell our politicians that enough is enough.

If we do not change these policies and practices then we will be left with another intergenerational legacy of trauma similar to the Stolen Generations. There has been more than enough warning that Australia is doing the wrong thing. How many times will we, as a nation, have to say sorry?

Chapter 54

LOVING AND LETTING GO

Back in 2016, when he was in Year Eleven, Abdul went on a two-week outdoor education expedition to the Nullarbor to camp and explore the hidden caves in the desert. Ironically, the Nullarbor is where Abdul saw his first live camel! Later I could see how this adventure had consolidated relationships with friends and teachers and had instilled confidence that he could make a life for himself in Australia.

Now that Abdul was out of community detention and his shoulder was better, he straight away proceeded to catch up on the adventures and challenges that healthy teenagers need. His school outdoor education program played a key role in this. As well as the Nullarbor trip, Abdul has been away kayaking, snorkelling, snowboarding, mountain biking and jumping down waterfalls.

But I miss him terribly when he is gone. The realisation that he will probably be the first child I need to practise letting go of as he sets off on his own hits me hard. I find myself missing the times we never had together. One of the most wonderful parts of parenthood is being able to share the beauty of the world with your young children. I am thankful that Abdul and Ahad had this connection and love with their own family in Afghanistan despite the war and trauma.

I know that letting go, not just physically but emotionally, is important so children can learn to do things on their own. Jasper taught me this when he was only three. We were at the pool and I was encouraging him to swim back to the edge as he had been doing in his swimming lessons.

'What's the matter, bub?' I asked him. 'Why aren't you swimming? I know you can do it.'

'Mummy, you have to let go of me. You're holding on too much.'

I still catch myself doing things like grabbing my boys' hands while we are waiting to cross the road.

Abdul has only been with me for a short time and my heart sometimes says he's still a baby. After these brief two years, it still seems to me that he should only be taking his first steps, not walking away.

xxxxxxx

Letting go requires a great deal of love. Letting go requires optimism about a future that could be secure. To love is to have hope.

One evening, Abdul and I stayed up by the fire after everyone else had gone to bed. We talked late into the night and he told me more about his life in Afghanistan.

Summer, he explained, is the murdering season because winters are far too harsh and difficult for the terrorists to make big attacks. The Taliban and other groups are so brainwashed with racism and violence that they would not think twice about killing people like Abdul and Ahad because they are Hazara. Because of this everyday savagery, people need to plan everything they do: even the most mundane and basic tasks, such as shopping, can be life-threatening. In such a place, lives are constricted and it is hard to aspire to anything more than survival.

'Someone might want to help others and make a change,' Abdul said. 'For example, studying for years to be a doctor. But then the next day he'll be shot in the street for nothing. It is all such a waste.'

Because of the government's failure to protect them, most Hazaras, including Abdul, have no faith that the Afghan government, the United Nations or any other external force will ever solve the crisis.

'I should be there, doing something,' he said. 'Even if I get killed. I could save someone.'

I know that he is torn because he is living here in safety while others, including his family, are exposed to danger. But the discussion was beginning to scare me, and I said, 'But returning and sacrificing yourself to save others would be futile.' I was also worried that this sort of talk was probably going to bring back nightmares and another sleepless week. I didn't want to see him spiral down into despair again or, worse, forget his dreams of a better life in Australia and return to Afghanistan.

I dearly wanted to make things better for Abdul, but that night we couldn't see any solution to decades of genocide and terror. There is no simple solution anyway. Maybe he thought I was too naive when I said there was still hope for peace, but I did believe that things would change one day. In my lifetime, there has been much bloodshed across the world. The Troubles in Northern Ireland, the Bosnian war and the Rwandan genocide have, to some extent, settled. I am in no position to claim that people are now happily living together, but things have improved.

In Australia, Aboriginal people were hunted down and there were mass killings by the European invaders. Later, children were stolen from their parents to make their Aboriginality disappear. This genocide was made possible by denying the humanity of Aboriginal people. Even now, the consequences of this trauma and racism continue to be reflected in the high incarceration rate of Aboriginal youths, unabated black deaths in custody, and the gap in mortality rates between Aboriginal Australians and the rest of the population. Despite all of this, Aboriginal people have survived, and identity and culture have not succumbed. There is always a flame of hope.

I knew it wasn't fair to declare to Abdul that things can change when his family remained in such danger and people were still dying. For Abdul, this was not an intellectual exercise to be studied from the comfort of our warm fireplace and then forgotten about the next day. This was real and it was an urgent matter of safety.

And yet these world problems also can't be solved by one passionate eighteen-year-old boy. Bravery and strength do not solve all problems. Abdul's mother sent him here because there was hope in Australia.

'Maybe, Abdul, you can fight in a different way.'

In his darkest moments, like that night, I needed him to remember that there was good in this world and what was worth pursuing now was education. With education, he would be able to do so much more than sacrifice his body. He could learn skills to help in peacemaking, rebuilding economies or healing and, in time, when the killings stop, Abdul could use his studies to help his people back in Afghanistan. The force that drove his mother to send her sons here is what makes humans endure despite the worst. Love, hope and the ability to let go because of faith in the future allows our survival in the face of all odds.

Chapter 55

WADBILLIGA

Now that Abdul's shoulder had healed, he and I planned to take off into the wilderness on our bikes. The other boys were not interested in biking for days without wi-fi in remote locations—most people aren't. Of course, Rob would have been a willing teammate, being a seasoned bike traveller. He has done some epic rides in North America and before we had kids we had journeyed together too. Abdul and Rob had some trips planned together in the future, but this time someone needed to stay at home with the rest of the boys.

It's a wonderful feeling to set off on two wheels, with legs fresh and well fuelled, bike panniers packed and firmly tied down, and the road beckoning ahead. On this day, in the summer of 2017, our destination was Wadbilliga National Park, a wilderness part of the southern Great Dividing Range.

We rode along four-wheel-drive fire trails through the mountain ranges near Cooma and aimed to eventually reach the coast. One thing about fire trails is that they tend to run over the top of mountains, presumably to aid the fight against the fires, whereas a travellers' road meanders through the valleys or follows the animal trails along the flat contour lines.

It was a massive challenge to get our bikes up and down some of the elevations, but this was also part of the adventure. We experienced the gradient of the mountains and heard the birds and insects and the wind blowing through the vegetation. Each pocket of bush had a different perfume of leaves and flowers, and even the scent of the rocks and clay lent complexity to the aroma.

Abdul and I had been on our bikes for five hours in 38-degree heat. A strong breeze high up on the mountain ridges was bending the tree trunks and dropping branches, which worried us. The bush seemed cowed by the ferocity of the heavy, relentless temperature. In truth, I had thrown my bike down in disgust and had been walking it, complaining, for the last hour. I had, of course, come down with a good dose of heat stroke and wanted to just push on to get to our goal. I was not thinking clearly so Abdul took over, suggesting we have an early lunch and drink the rest of our water. A little later we arrived at a creek, but we were a long way from anywhere, and a long way from help if we needed it.

Still, we cheered with gratitude and sat in the creek to cool off—there would be no more riding today. More refreshed, we wheeled our bikes along the creek edge, lifting them over fallen tree limbs and past clumps of prickly bursaria as we searched for a camp spot. The creek, with a steep forest slope on one side and lightly wooded grassland on the other, bubbled over a bed of round rocks. A warm breeze blew in our faces: not pleasant, but better than no breeze at all.

Once we set up camp, we sat under one of the big casuarinas leaning over the creek, its long, needle-like leaves making a pattern of lace in the shade. Further down the creek were towering ribbon gums with smooth white trunks festooned with long strands of trailing bark and massive angophoras with grey gnarled limbs like something out of a fairytale.

The sun-dappled water was clear but tinged with tannin. As a crowd of backswimmers circled, sparks of light flashed like yellow diamonds, and tiny fish with no caution whatsoever nibbled at my feet when I dipped them into the water.

The afternoon was spent watching the goings-on in that corner of the bush. From the steep cliff opposite came a sound of snapping twigs and a clutter of rocks signalling where a small water dragon had fallen clumsily down the scree slope. Two small, golden whistler birds flew down from the branches of the casuarina and hopped back and forth on the small branches above our heads. A kingfisher with a copper chest and bright-blue head landed on a partly submerged branch on the other side of the creek, before skimming the surface in a long swoop and disappearing out of sight around the bend. A solitary black wallaby hopped down the slope and picked through the grass, oblivious to our presence, while a large goanna circled our tent and then ran up a tree, where he watched us in stillness.

I tapped Abdul's leg, then I tapped again more urgently. I didn't want to startle him. A red-bellied black snake was swimming towards us with its small, perfect head held elegantly out of the water. It climbed the bank a few metres from us, scales glistening, and looked around. After rolling on the grass—I have no idea why it did that—it returned to the creek's edge and lay motionless on the stones.

I looked over at Abdul, who was immersed in the beauty around him, and reflected on how he had become more connected with the land and the bush than most people whose families had lived here for generations.

That evening, we marvelled at what we had seen while we had a lovely meal, made with whatever we could carry on our bikes and no cooking facilities. We talked until late, using the conversation to make sure we kept on drinking water, before heading off to bed.

Soon after midnight I woke feeling dreadful. The earth was spinning and powerful waves of nausea rolled over me whenever I moved my head. Vertigo, I thought. It can last for days, but I was also worried about food poisoning or, worse, if I was sick from the drinking water. But most likely I was still feeling the effects of the heat stroke.

Abdul looked after me through the night, fetching more water and providing comfort, and by the morning the vertigo and nausea had improved to the extent that I could stand up. If I moved around too much, though, it all came back.

Abdul insisted that he ride his bike back up the mountain, fetch our car and come to get me. I had considered riding back with him, but it was still too hot and there would be a lot more uphill, so the going would be even tougher than yesterday. I worried about the car making it, because our four-wheel drive had already blown a tyre on the journey to the start of the ride and there was no second spare. To return, Abdul would be driving downhill on the rocky terrain on the skimpy spare and there was no room for further mishaps. Weighing up these challenges, I reluctantly conceded we had little choice but for Abdul to go.

He set off on his bike with six litres of water, food and, most importantly, the car keys. While he was slogging his way uphill, I spent the next few hours sitting in the shade with my feet dangling in the gurgling creek, thankful for this place. Getting up to stretch my legs, I found a perfect eagle feather in the grass, and with this I knew that we would be okay.

Each week I had seen the capacity, tenacity and equanimity of this young man grow. I thought about how many different environments, and how many different roles, Abdul had had to take on in the last few years and don't know many others who could have been as adaptable. I was grateful for all that strength and perseverance as it has allowed him to survive.

Late that afternoon, just before sunset, I heard a rumbling from across the mountainside. I scrambled along the edge of the creek to the road and saw the familiar shape of my white car coming down the track, with Abdul smiling at the wheel. He got out of the car and we high-fived it. After a cup of tea, we packed up camp and headed home.

Chapter 56

HOPE

Abdul had the bare minimum of schooling in Afghani-stan. He had learned to read and write in Dari and had a few years of arithmetic. He was lucky to be able to read and write in his first language, and these built a foundation for his learning in English. Abdul saw the silver lining in the deten-tion cloud as an opportunity to study. Not only did he attend English classes at school, he also spent every spare minute practising. He would talk to the guards, the police officers assigned to the camps as community liaisons and anyone else. It was all an opportunity to improve his English.

In Darwin, the detention kids went to school in a Serco minivan for their three-hour school day. While they had lessons the guards stood outside the classroom. Once on Facebook I asked Abdul if he had made any friends with Aussie kids.

He told me they never saw any Australian students when at Sanderson High in Darwin because they were segregated.

Abdul was affronted that during the first six months of school in Canberra he was required to go to ESL classes rather than join the rest of the mainstream subjects. He so wanted to be involved and to belong. He believed his English was good enough. And his spoken English *was* good, but what he needed to learn was how to write reasoned essays. His first year in Canberra was to catch up, as best as he could, on ten years of missed education.

Starting Year Eleven at a new school in 2016, Abdul was keen to work hard in order to get a place at university. But there were times when I saw a dark cloud descending and his positivity and impetus to study evaporated. These episodes were usually related to something terrible happening in Afghanistan, or when he was reminded of his vulnerability in Australia. His whole demeanour changed.

'What's the point?' he would say when I asked why he had not gone to school. 'They can send me back any day. All the years I've been here are just wasted time.'

How hard is it to keep on studying in Year Eleven for something that you may not be allowed to do even if you have the marks?

'You're on the way to getting the marks for university,' I told him. 'You're almost there. Even if they send you back to Afghanistan, you'll have this education you can put to use.'

In my heart, I couldn't believe he would be sent back, but I was not entirely optimistic about his chances of being allowed to study at university. It would not be helpful to join him in a spiral of catastrophe so the only thing that we could do was, as Winston Churchill said, 'keep buggering on'.

Abdul wanted to become a high school teacher and I reckoned he was on to something. With his energy, his humour, his ready smile and natural leadership, he would be a fantastic teacher. He also had street smarts and an edge that could really inspire the most reluctant and wayward students to engage with him.

xxxxxxx

In late January 2017, Abdul left for Brisbane to spend time with Ahad, who was still working as a painter, and to visit his extended relatives' network. After a few days when I did not hear from him, I called, and Abdul told me that he wasn't coming back to Canberra. He had decided to stay in Brisbane. If he couldn't go to university, then there was no point continuing school, and if the government was going to kick him out soon, he would rather spend his remaining time with his brother. My heart felt like it had dropped 1000 metres from the sky, but Abdul's decision was not unexpected.

After 14 months of waiting on a bridging visa, Abdul had lost hope. He couldn't go to university without the five-year SHEV, and the three-year TFV would not allow him to study. Worse yet, the department could decide that he was not a refugee after all, meaning he would most likely be sent back into detention onshore or on Christmas Island awaiting deportation back to Afghanistan.

I was beside myself. All of us loved Abdul and we didn't want him to leave in this way. But I was also worried that he was throwing away his chances by quitting school with only one year to go. I could not persuade him to return. With the new school year starting in a few days, I asked one of his teachers to help.

'How are you going, mate?' Dan, his outdoor education teacher, asked over the phone.

Abdul replied that he was okay but he was choosing to stay in Brisbane and get a job because it was time he should support himself.

'Fair enough,' Dan responded. 'You know what you are doing. But is there anything we can do to help? Could the school write to immigration?'

'That's been done . . . heaps,' Abdul said, and told Dan about the long campaign I had waged on his behalf.

'Okay. You know what you are doing and I know you have to make the right decision for yourself.'

After the call, Abdul knew that more people than he had expected genuinely cared and that he had a place and a life back in Canberra too.

Almost a week later, immigration left a message for Abdul, but he didn't return their call. He also missed several messages from his lawyer. Some days later, a lawyer from RACS asked me to get Abdul to call. I was hopeful about this development, but Abdul wasn't.

'Abdul, you never know, it could be good news. Please call immigration.'

'There is no good news from them,' he replied.

I insisted and eventually Abdul called. He was sitting in a McDonald's in suburban Brisbane waiting for Ahad to finish a painting job when he found out that he had been granted a visa. 'Can I study?' was the first question he asked. Yes, he could! Abdul had been granted the SHEV, which meant that he could stay for another five years and, most importantly, he could go to university.

When a large, official envelope arrived in the mail, it became real. Abdul had his SHEV, which finally acknowledged that he was a refugee. Yet from Brisbane, Abdul was subdued. He was not ungrateful, but after all he had been dragged through—after three and a half years of limbo, after being imprisoned as an innocent person for seventeen months, after having his personal details leaked onto the internet by immigration—it seemed too little, too late. Much of this pain could have been avoided, and the reality still remained that the SHEV was only a temporary visa, with no assurance that Abdul would have a future beyond the five years. 'They will never make it easy,' he told me.

The real celebration came when Abdul returned home. He flew back unannounced one day when we were all out at work and school. I didn't know he was home until he came down from his bedroom and gave me a hug.

'I'm home again', he said brightly. Despite the visa not being greeted with the jubilation some may have expected, what it did do was give Abdul the impetus to begin Year Twelve. If he had not got this visa, it would have been a disaster. There was no recourse to challenge in the new Fast-Track system and he would not have been allowed to work or study, and he would not have been allowed government assistance. Without us, he would have been left destitute.

Having a SHEV made it possible for Abdul to study at university. There was also a theoretical possibility that he may later be eligible to apply for a skilled work visa after graduating. But the cruel fact is that, with so many barriers, even this is made impossible for most refugees. Although SHEV holders can study at university, they can only do so as international students, paying their fees upfront. To give an idea of the costs involved, annual university fees for international students in a Bachelor of Arts at the ANU in 2018 were $40,416, and a similar degree at the University of Canberra costs $25,400 a year. There is a ticking clock for refugees to pay these substantial tertiary fees, support themselves financially and get their qualifications in the five-year period.

'I can only study if I get a full scholarship,' Abdul said. He had begun to worry. 'And what if I can't get one? What's the point of trying so hard when I can't go to university anyway.'

'Abdul, you know I'm happy to pay the fees,' I said. I'm lucky that I'm a doctor and can earn enough to support Abdul in this way. 'The other boys will have to pay uni fees, too. When they finish, they will pay the government back. When you finish, you'll pay me instead.'

'But what if I'm sent to Afghanistan and I can't pay you back?'

That fear was always at the back of his mind. Still, I suspected the main reason behind his reluctance to have me pay was his pride. Understandably, he didn't want to be beholden to us for the financial costs of his studies, but I didn't want him to give up if he didn't get a scholarship. To me, it was worth paying the money to get him through.

'Well, I'll have to take that risk,' I continued. 'There is no way you can work enough hours to support yourself and earn enough money to pay your fees. There won't be enough hours in the day after that to learn anything.'

He replied with silence.

'Abdul, we've got this far, I want to help you. If you don't get a scholarship, please let me help by lending you the money. In the meantime, go to school please.'

I had to use all my energy to encourage this boy to keep on when he felt so empty. With Abdul's only chance of long-lasting freedom in Australia being through education, it was going to be a marathon effort.

✕✕✕✕✕✕✕

In the years that have passed since Abdul arrived, I am noticing a change in the relationship between him and my three boys. We have grown as a family in this time and the boys have also grown and changed, too, as different phases of teenagehood pass us by.

Abdul has told me he has noticed things that his Australian brothers have done recently that show how much they care about him. When Abdul's aunt and cousin came to visit, Jasper looked after them all as the host, and when it was Abdul's turn to cook dinner for everyone and he struggled with an adventurous recipe, Lucas helped him get through it, while only the other day Toby told Abdul, 'I'm so glad you're here because we can do more adventures with you.'

Chapter 57

THE MOUNTAIN–AN ALLEGORY

Time is not linear. Yes, time progresses, but there are days when old conflicts and problems circle back to haunt us. Over the last few years, there have been many beautiful moments, but it has been hard, too, and despite my trying to ignore it, a storm had been brewing inside of me.

A lifetime of being responsible and working for others had been weighing down on me. When I finished school, I went straight to university. I married young and divorced in my medical intern year, and I continued to work as I got my life back together. Then I met Rob. We married, we studied together for our specialist exams, and then we had kids. I was a cliché: the high-achieving eldest daughter, the accommodating friend, the doctor whose time is infinite, and the juggling everything mum. I knew I was burning out, but too many people depended on me.

There had been so much going on. My boys were good kids, but they still needed my time and attention. I had been trying to support all my friends, and I was still worrying about what was going to happen to Abdul. At work, I noticed that I had been feeling others' pain and fear far more than before, but at the same time I felt a deadening inside me. It was not just one thing or another doing this, but a constant trickle making an ever-deeper pool that threatened to drown me. I was maxed out and it made me horrid and needy, and I carped on and nagged at everyone at home.

The things I used to do to fill my reserves now seemed too hard to even think about, let alone give any time to. I had isolated myself from many friends, especially groups, because groups seemed more like work than fun. Not surprisingly, I felt alone. I was still running a bit, and taking steps to get my workload down to a reasonable level by cutting down on clinics and hospital inpatient work so I could get my weekends back. I'd learned that it was easier not to ask for help at home because I couldn't tolerate the four boys' grumpy lack of willingness. I'd also had a gutful of being needed. I had nothing left inside to give.

On the outside, I was still doing and saying the right things. I kept my struggles to myself because that has been a lifelong way to cope. I knew I wasn't a very fun person to be around, but the truth was I just wanted to be left alone. It seemed that I had stopped breathing; I knew that if I truly breathed out, a flood of tears would follow.

Rob and I used to go on amazing adventures together: bike expeditions, camping, kayaking, travelling. Where did that escape go? But each day on my way to work, I had started to look out to the mountains in the distance with urgency. I wanted to run away.

I still loved Rob, but I was hard on him. We had simply forgotten to give ourselves time together and I missed him even though he was right there. He was in the background being an admirable husband, working, providing, doing the cooking, listening and, all the while, loving me. But when I got tired or upset or distracted, he withdrew, guessing that I wanted space when what I really needed was him. I also wanted him to see past all the 'good' things I was doing and adore the real me underneath, even when I wasn't nice. I also wanted him to see that I was lonely; I wanted him to gather me in to him. But by this stage, because I had been so horrid, I was afraid he might not want to do this even if I had asked.

I was not just missing my husband. I was missing my boys. When they were little, we hugged and danced and played. Tucking them into bed, they would ask, 'Mummy for a little while?' This was the best, lying in the dark, snuggled in with my beautiful sons, telling stories and chatting. In fact, looking back, these were probably the best moments of my life. I would do anything for a taste of that again. But those little boys had gone. At a certain stage of their teen years, they had each renounced spontaneous cuddles. They didn't want to be my babies again and this was how it had to be. My job was to support my sons in finding their own paths to becoming men. It also meant that when I suggested another expedition or holiday, none of them wanted to go with me; they preferred to be at home, close to wi-fi. The only person keen to be an 'adventure buddy' was Abdul.

Almost a year after the Wadbilliga trip, I planned another venture with him. I thought that twelve days driving to Uluru would be the solution to getting me out of my rut. We planned the route, and I had organised for my clinic to be closed, until Abdul announced there had been a miscommunication. He had never agreed to go. He had organised a holiday job instead.

Maybe he had been freaked out by my neediness, but in my vulnerable state of mind Abdul's rejection touched a nerve. Certainly, my extreme hurt and disappointment when he told me should have been a flashing alarm that something was terribly wrong.

What I thought I wanted was to be wanted—not because of what people needed from me but because I was fun to be with. I wanted people to want to hang out with me because of me. I wanted to be light and frolicsome and unafraid again. But I wasn't any of those things anymore.

Maybe being in the bush on my own would give me back my strength. So I took off to a mountain. The destination was Gibraltar Peak in Tidbinbilla National Park, just outside Canberra, an important and distinctive place with huge granite tors. I walked the crunching dirt road through native pasture, then turned right along the narrow trail winding up through the bush gully. It was spring and supposed to be a time of bright green shoots and growth, but in the drought the delicate native ferns had either become a sickly leathery olive colour or had died. Along the dry creek bed, the invading European blackberry was getting the upper hand. This land was struggling, like my spirit.

As I looked up to my mountain destination, I saw that the sky had turned black. In my preoccupation, I had not noticed the approaching storm before I set off. A few drops of rain fell and a warm, earthy scent surrounded me. Two Australian scientists in the 1960s discovered that rainfall causes rocks to release aerosols of a yellowish oil responsible for this odour that they called *petrichor*, which means 'blood of rocks'. To me, *petrichor* smells like optimism and reassurance.

The raindrops plopped more insistently and rumbles from the sky shook the ground. The *petrichor* had gone and now the sharp tang of ozone replaced it. As I felt the charge of electricity building in the air around me, I realised that what I was doing—walking up a mountain during a lightning storm—was unsafe. I jogged up to a rock shelter I knew was there and reached it just in time: the storm then rapidly worsened. As I crouched between the boulders, dripping wet, trying to find a space to avoid the rivers of water rushing down the rock face, I was glad that I had packed a thermos of tea, which I poured between shivers, clasping the warm mug in my hands.

The sky sparked with flashes of lightning and the thunder replied each time with growing frequency. One heavy crash just nearby made me flinch and I hoped that this was not the one moment in millions of years when lightning would smash apart the boulders I had sheltered under. I was cold and scared, alone and homesick. Then a hailstorm clattered down, building up into drifts of ice.

Finally, when the storm quietened into a steady downpour of rain, I took the chance to get down off the mountain as quickly as I could by running down the slippery path. Skidding on a patch of wet clay and hailstones, I slipped and my left side hit the ground hard. Lying there in pain, I thought to myself, *Well, this is just stupid.* And, to put the boot in further, *You deserve this.* It was my fault I got myself into this situation because I had ignored the danger signals for too long. A thought crossed my mind that I could lie here forever. That I could just give up. There was no fight or instinct or purpose left.

The rain kept on coming. As it washed the mud off my legs and my face, I realised that this rain was needed; the land needed it and maybe I needed this storm on the mountain to realise what was important to me. I pulled myself up and made my way back to the car.

When I limped into our house some time later, shaking with cold and wet through, Rob looked at me, slightly amused.

'Had a good run, then?'

When my look told him it hadn't been, he bundled me up in his warm arms and held me until I was finally able to exhale. I realised that I had never seen that Rob had been there all the time. The storm had passed and I had found my husband again.

XXXXXXX

This, of course, is not the end of the story: that we lived happily ever after. Rob and I needed to do much more to reconnect, but now I could see how we could. We had been

315

too busy and preoccupied by everyone else's needs to recognise how we had been slipping away from each other. Our relationship could not be rebuilt with one hug. We needed to start talking and *seeing* each other again. And that would take time and it would not always be easy. Luckily both he and I are good at endurance. We had endured through our three, and then with Abdul and Ahad. Now it was time for us.

Chapter 58

HAPPINESS

Coming in from work in the dark tonight I find the house warm and well lit. The aroma of roast chicken and potatoes is welcoming. Just after me is Jasper, home from uni on his bike, and inside he explains the day's science lectures with enthusiasm. Rob is still wearing his sweaty bike gear as he too has only just arrived home. He is serving up the dinner that Lucas has prepared. I give him a kiss.

Abdul helps out by fetching Toby to the table: at fourteen, Toby has to be pried away from messaging the friends with whom he has spent all day at school. While Abdul has the knack of cheerfully doing this, it often results in several minutes of wrestling around the lounge room before the boys can settle to dinner. I don't mind at all. They're having fun, and Toby has no hope of putting Abdul on the ground. But he persists again and again, getting sweatier as the volume of laughs and exclamations crescendos. These few minutes of chaos allow everyone to reach dinner relaxed.

When Lucas sees Abdul make a beeline for the kettle, he puts his hands on his hips and says in a comically exasperated voice, 'Oh, Abdul, you and your tea!'

'Yes, my friend,' Abdul replies. 'Do you want some?' *My friend* is the current stock phrase in our household.

At the dinner table, Lucas is a natural mimic, and loud and funny. We occasionally suggest that he shut down the monologue, which I think sounds like the soundtrack of a cartoon program, but the truth is I don't want him to. Lucas is fizzing with energy and this creates a fun atmosphere. There is some verbal jostling between the boys, but it is all good-natured.

This afternoon I spoke with Ahad on the phone. He recently got the news that he is getting his Australian citizenship. If Abdul had arrived in Australia just a few days earlier, before 19 July 2013, he could have also had this possibility. But I can't let that mar our happiness and excitement for Ahad.

At the table, Jasper and Abdul exchange a wry eye roll when I say something that is apparently too motherly and daggy. Talking about daggy, Abdul is wearing his bright-yellow lifeguard uniform: his new part-time jobs are as a lifeguard and swimming teacher. I have no doubt he will be a star at this because he has a lovely way with kids. It is wonderful that a boy who arrived on a boat, unable to swim, is giving back to the community in this way. He has also got back into

Happiness

some training for boxing and wrestling, and together with
Rob he has cleared out a space in the garage and set up a gym
that both of them use.

The years have passed quickly since I first met Abdul in
detention. In spite of all the challenges that have been put
in his way, I know he will succeed. He is now studying for
a Certificate III in Outdoor Education, and next year he
intends to study at university, with good options for a scholarship. Both will help his goals to become a high school teacher.
There is hope for him staying in Australia long-term and we
need to focus on this; Abdul, as well as tens of thousands
of other refugees, could still be made to leave Australia at
the end of their visas. This uncertainty is intolerable and
sometimes, in order to survive, like tonight, it needs to be
forgotten. The solution is not in the hands of these asylum
seekers and refugees. Instead it is up to everyday people in
Australia to inform our government that this unfair treatment
of humans is unacceptable. This is the only way that policies
will change.

Soon all the boys have left the table and it is just Rob and
me sitting across from each other in the quiet. We realise
that we are happy. Happiness is not just the excitement of
special things happening or a special occasion. This is a
quiet and calm happiness that is as complete as any we have
had, and it has snuck up on us. Possibly we are more able to
see it now we have passed through most of the worries and
challenges of the last few years.

Of course, there will be more trials with our boys. Of
course, that doesn't mean that we won't argue tomorrow

... or even later tonight. Happiness isn't a thing that you deliberately create to be kept forever. Happiness is found in recognising these fleeting moments.

A blessing has descended on us and we are grateful. Our family has grown. We are together and we care for each other. There is acceptance and there is hope. And, for the next few years, we are all safe.

AFTERWORD

'Whatever you did for one of these least brothers and sisters of mine, you did for me.'

Matthew 25:40

There are too many voiceless babies and children who have been labelled illegal and have spent too many years of their short lives behind barbed wire. Even if they have been released, they are still without hope of a stable future. These children have been subjected to a profoundly abnormal and toxic situation in detention centres, which will certainly leave long-term psychological and physical damage in the name of 'stopping the boats'.

There is no evidence that punishing asylum seekers in this way stops boats or prevents drownings at sea. Unfortunately, politicians believe that it gets votes from the public, most of whom do not understand or want to know what damage is being done in our name.

We need to keep these children in our minds. If we stand up for kindness and decency, these kids and their parents may have a chance. If each person who now knows what is happening could tell their politicians that these policies are not acceptable, then the situation would change. Politicians do care: they care most fundamentally about votes.

xxxxxxx

This book started as a security plan for Abdul. I had hoped that if enough people knew about Abdul's situation, then maybe the government would not continue their shameful treatment of people seeking safety, with Abdul, in particular, being allowed to stay here.

Abdul does not want to be defined by the word *refugee*. No one does. Abdul is not just a boy who survived a bomb explosion, or drowning at sea. And while he was almost broken by immigration detention, his spirit saved him. Abdul has soared above the clouds and he has survived.

He has so much to give to our country—if he is allowed. Abdul told me this recently, and it's a message of optimism for everyone:

'I am older now. You let me be younger so I could catch up, but from now on it is my turn to help you when you need it.'

ACKNOWLEDGEMENTS

There are so many people I would like to thank.

My dearest husband, Rob, above all others.

This book is intended as a gift to all my boys. I love you. I hope, maybe in years to come, that you understand what I was trying to achieve for all of you. My sons Jasper, Lucas and Toby, who have been so kind, gracious and real: I am glad I have grown young men that Australia should be proud of. I am bursting with pride and love for all of you. And Abdul and Ahad: I believe we have always been connected. Because of a series of impossibilities, we didn't know that until it was almost too late. Thank you for your bravery in agreeing to be part of this book.

Ahad, I miss you. I wish we could hug and that we could look into each other's eyes with the pain gone. You might think I don't care, but that is not true. I ran out of knowing what to do and I was scared to chase you anymore.

My dearest Abdul, I understand now how hard it is to find the right words. I love you.

Thank you to my parents, my friends who sustain me, to my lovely sister-in-law, Alice. And thank you to all the others who have helped the boys along the way. Some we know, others we may never know, but we owe you our gratitude. And thank you to the unknown school mum who stayed with Lucas when he needed help.

I have written each word of this book as a newbie, and many times I have felt the truth of what Hemingway described as 'all you do is sit down at a typewriter and bleed'. I have benefitted from the support of many people. Gaby Naher, who gave me a chance, and Kelly Fagan at Allen & Unwin, who encouraged me and brought it all together. My thanks to Denise Leith, for her mentorship. And my thanks to the editing sleuths at Allen & Unwin, Angela Handley and especially Rebecca Starford, whose feedback had me grumbling inside at first but, truly, I am very thankful and grateful for their wisdom and skill.

To the immigration staff, the guards, the case workers and the health professionals who did try to help and support Abdul—I give you my heartfelt thanks.

And those who have helped from their hearts and minds: Justine Davis, Sophie Peer, Georgie Nutton, Professor Caroline de Costa, Brian Kelleher, Father Nikolai Blaskow, Father Richard Browning, Professor Alan Rosen, Professor William Maley, Julian Burnside AO QC and the late Mr Malcolm Fraser AC CH GCL.